Boat Handling
Under Power

D1508909

Also by John Mellor

Sailing Can Be Simple
Cruising Safe and Simple
The Motor Cruising Manual
* The Sailing Cruiser Manual
* The Art of Pilotage

and contributions to

The Best of SAIL Cruising
The Best of SAIL Navigation

* Also published by Sheridan House

BOAT HANDLING UNDER POWER

A Motorboat and Yacht Owners' Guide

JOHN MELLOR

SHERIDAN HOUSE

Published by Sheridan House Inc.
145 Palisade Street
Dobbs Ferry, NY 10522

First paperback edition 1993
Reprinted 1994, 1996, 1999

Library of Congress Cataloging-in-Publication Data
Mellor, John.
   Boat handling under power: a motorboat and yacht owners' guide /
John Mellor.—1st pbk. ed.
     p.   cm.
   ISBN 0–924486–43–0: $16.50
    1. Seamanship. 2. Boats and boating. I. Title.
VK543.M38 1993
623.88—dc20   92–41636
                                   CIP

Printed in Great Britain

ISBN 0-924486-43-0

For Caroline and family and the Varuna

Thanks to Mike Bellamy of Lancing Marine for technical advice on propellers

Contents

8 Stability and Sails

9 Handling at Sea

10 Special Handling Techniques

11 Breakdowns and Bad Weather

Appendix

Foreword

Handling a boat well under power is no less of a challenge to a skipper than handling one well under sail. In certain respects it is more difficult, due to the complex interactions of the forces involved. Although experience is a fine medium for honing a skipper's ability to a keen edge, it is of little use without a thorough understanding of these forces and their effects.

In this book we are going to discuss these forces and the ways in which they can be best used when handling a boat under power—be she a large twin-screw motor yacht or a smaller sailing boat with an outboard auxiliary. In order that we may concentrate on detailed, and in some cases quite difficult, techniques, the reader is assumed to possess some basic knowledge and experience of boats, their machinery and general seamanship.

A good craftsman of any sort first learns precisely how his tools work, before he ever begins using them. We must do the same.

1 Propulsion and Steering

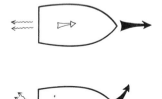

In essence, we can say that a boat under power is propelled by a stream of water ejected from her stern by a propeller; and is steered by directing this *slipstream* to one side so as to push the stern across and realign her in the required direction (fig. 1). Although, as we shall see, propulsion and steering are rather more complex than this, and there are many things that affect these basic facts, this simple statement illustrated in (1) always holds good, and should be remembered. A boat is controlled under power by moving her stern around, and all propulsion and steering systems should be considered in the light of the effect they have on the stern of a boat, not on her bow.

1 **Effect of slipstream**

Propulsion

It can be constructive to imagine a propeller as a sort of screw (which is precisely what it originally was) that winds its way through the water, pushing the boat before it. In an ideal world this is just what would happen. The world, however, is not ideal—it is hard work pushing a boat forward, and difficult for a screw to get a grip in something as soft as water. The poor old propeller, although trying very hard to grip the water and push the boat forwards, ends up gripping the boat and pushing the water backwards. It battles on like this for a while until the thrust of its slip-stream overcomes the inertia of the boat and starts her moving. As the boat moves, so the prop gradually gets a firmer grip on the water, and the slipstream it pushes astern of the boat diminishes as it increasingly begins to actually wind its way through the water.

A propulsion system, then, has two basic effects: it pushes the boat one way, and it pushes water the other, the degree of each effect depending on how difficult the boat is to push. If the boat is light, slim, powerful or already moving in the right direction, slipstream will be minimal and thrust considerable. If she is heavy, fat, stopped, under-powered, or currently moving in the wrong direction, slip-stream will be considerable and thrust minimal. These are extremely important factors in the handling of a boat under power, as we shall see.

Steering

There are two basic ways of angling this slipstream to one side so as to push the stern across and steer the boat. One is to swivel the prop in order to eject the slipstream directly away from where it is required to push the stern—the method employed with outboards and outdrives (fig. 2). The other is to hang a rudder behind the prop, so that when turned it deflects the slipstream (fig. 3).

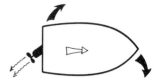

2 **Swivelling prop directing slipstream**

It should be immediately apparent from a comparison of diagrams (2) and (3) that the former is the more efficient, as it angles all the slipstream in the desired direction, rather than the half that is diverted by a rudder. Furthermore, when the boat is going astern the fully swivelling propeller will steer just as efficiently as it does when going ahead (fig. 4). The rudder, however, will hardly steer at all going astern as the slipstream will be pushed forward—away from it.

On the other hand, if the boat is moving through the water and the propeller is stopped, there will be no slipstream and the swivelling propeller cannot steer, either ahead or astern. The water flowing past the boat, however, can be diverted by an angled rudder whether going ahead or astern, and this diverted water flow will act like the slipstream, pushing the stern to one side (fig. 5).

3 **Rudder deflecting slipstream**

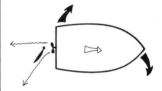

The faster the flow of water ejected to one side of the stern, the more rapidly the boat will turn—whether this is caused by the slipstream from a swivelling prop or over a rudder, or by water flowing past a boat and over a rudder.

Propeller Effects

Though for simplicity we can liken it to a screw, a propeller is actually rather complex. We mentioned above the difficulty a prop has in actually getting a boat moving through the water, and how much more easily it works when she is steadily under way. It should be apparent that a propeller suitable for starting off a heavy displacement boat and then pushing her along at 8 knots is likely to have rather different design characteristics to one that will efficiently move off a very light planing boat, then push her along at 28 knots.

For efficiency, the design of a propeller needs to be very carefully matched to the shape and displacement of the boat it is to drive, and also to the power and maximum rpm of the power unit. Propulsion engineers can feed this information into a computer and have it design exactly the right prop for your boat. As different props produce varying effects at the stern of a boat, you should know something about these design parameters.

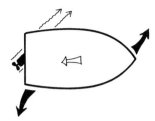

4 Swivelling prop, going astern

5 No power, but rudder deflecting water flow from ahead and astern

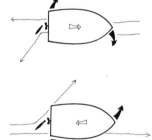

6 Conventional three-bladed prop

Diameter

This is the width of an imaginary circle centred on the boss of the propeller, that just encloses the tips of the blades. A heavy displacement boat generally requires a large diameter prop turning at slow speed, in order to overcome its inertia with the minimum of slip. The heavy and powerful engine that will produce such necessary torque is little hindrance to a boat like that. A light planing boat, however, needs a lightweight engine whose lack of torque will drive her most efficiently through a small diameter prop turning at high speed, due to the ease with which she can be pushed through the water. A fine-lined displacement boat will not need as large a prop as a fat, barge-like vessel, and can turn it faster with a higher-revving engine. In general, a large, slow-revving prop has the best grip on the water and produces least delay due to slip before moving the boat, although this will be affected by the shape and weight of the hull.

Pitch

A measure of the twist in a propeller blade, defined as the theoretical distance a propeller would screw forward in one revolution if it did not slip. It is similar in concept to the size of thread on a bolt or screw. It should be apparent that the greater (or coarser) the pitch of a prop, the harder it will be to turn, as one revolution must push the boat further than one revolution of a finer-pitched prop, displacing more water to do so.

The easier a boat is to push through the water, the coarser pitch her prop can have. The prop for a displacement boat will normally have a pitch somewhat smaller than its diameter, while that for a high-speed one will have a pitch rather larger. If a boat has too coarsely-pitched a prop, the engine will have difficulty in turning it. This will show up as an inability to reach the designed maximum rpm, and as clouds of black smoke from the exhaust if it is a diesel. If the pitch of the prop is too fine, it will not move the boat at the expected speed for the engine revolutions set, and maximum rpm may be exceeded if the engine is not governed.

Blades

The number and shape vary, but the most commonly encountered props have three 'clover-leaf' blades, as shown in fig. 6. Their shape produces efficient thrust, while the odd number reduces vibration, especially when the prop is working in disturbed water.

At low rotation speeds props with four or more blades are quieter and more efficient, the even numbers causing little vibration if the prop is working in undisturbed water away from the sternpost.

At very high rotation speeds, two-bladed props become efficient, and the inherent vibration can be reduced by shaping the blades like sickles, as on the high-speed outboard in fig. 7.

Two-bladed props with long thin blades are often found fitted to auxiliary sailing craft, the reduced resistance they offer when sailing being regarded as compensation for their inherent inefficiency (fig. 8). If the shaft is marked with the position of the blades, it can be rotated so as to reduce drag even further by aligning the blades with the sternpost or rudder when the engine is not in use.

Equipoise blades are lop-sided, as you can see on the outdrive in fig. 9. This gives extra blade area for a given diameter, thus creating the effect of a bigger, more powerful propeller.

Direction of rotation

For reasons that will become apparent, propellers are designed to drive a boat forward by rotating either clockwise or anti-clockwise (as viewed from astern). The former are known as *right-handed* and the latter *left-handed*. The significance of this is that as a prop revolves it does three basic things: it drives the boat forward; it throws out a slipstream astern; and, due to the twist in the blades, it tries to paddle across sideways (rather like a wheel) in the direction it is turning. If it is right-handed (turning clockwise) it will pull the stern to starboard when going ahead, and to port when going astern (when its direction of rotation is reversed). A left-handed prop will pull the other way round (fig. 10). This is known as *paddlewheel effect*, and it is often a major factor in the handling of a boat. The greater the inertia the prop is trying to overcome, the greater will be its paddlewheel effect. The result is that the effect varies in the same way, and for the same reasons, as slipstream. It is, however, also greater with large, slow-revving props than with small high-speed ones.

The handing of a propeller, and thus the direction of its paddlewheel effect, can be easily ascertained by watching which way round the shaft revolves when the boat is going ahead. It will also be found marked on the prop itself, together with the dimensions of pitch and diameter. A marking such as—24 × 15 LH— will indicate a left-handed propeller with a 24 in. diameter and 15 in. pitch, the relationship of diameter to pitch indicating that it belongs to a displacement boat. Looking at a prop and imagining it as a screw will tell you the way it turns: those in figs. 6 and 9 are left-handed, and in figs. 7 and 8 right-handed.

7 **Two-bladed high-speed prop**

8 **Two-bladed solid prop in position of least drag**

9 **Sterndrive (outdrive) with equipoise blades**

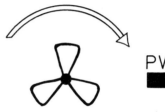

LH prop ahead

RH prop ahead

RH prop astern

LH prop astern

10 **Paddlewheel effect**

Steering Effects

Steering is also slightly more complex than has so far been intimated. Let us consider what happens when the helm is put over on a boat that is moving at steady speed.

The basic action of a rudder can be considered to have four distinct stages. First there is a pause before the diversion of the water flow actually begins to move the stern, its duration depending on the speed and displacement of the boat: the greater her momentum, the more time it will take her to answer her helm. As a rough guide we can say that a heavy boat at normal speed may carry on for a couple of lengths before starting to turn.

The second stage—the first actual effect of the rudder— is not to swing the stern but to cause the whole boat to drift bodily out of the turn. The amount of drift will depend on the resistance the hull presents to the water when moving sideways (the amount that is underwater) and the force that is pushing her sideways (her speed and weight). A deep long-keeled boat at slow speed will drift a good deal less than a shallow planing boat at high speed.

The third stage is a reduction in speed due to the drag of the rudder blade; the amount depends on the size of rudder and the angle to which it is turned. For these reasons rudders are carefully designed to be no larger than is necessary, and stops are normally fitted to prevent them being turned more than 35°, beyond which angle the drag becomes excessive. Certain vessels requiring the ability to turn very short round at slow speeds, such as large canal barges, have rudders that can swing the full 90°, the manoeuvring benefits from slipstream effect being more important than drag.

This speed reduction is fairly small except during long turns under full helm when travelling fast. Under such circumstances a displacement motor cruiser could lose up to a third of her original speed by the time she reaches a reciprocal course. If the turn is continued beyond this she will lose very little more, and when the rudder is straightened she will gradually resume her original speed.

The final effect of putting the rudder over is to actually swing the stern in the desired direction. It does not, however, pivot around the bow but around a point roughly one-third of the hull length back from it. This causes the bow to swing inside the turn as the stern swings out. However, if sideways drift is excessive, as with a shallow planing boat, the whole boat can slide right out of the turn, creating the effect of a pivot point actually well ahead of the bow (fig. 11).

If the rudder is put over when the boat is moving astern, the same effects occur. This time the bow swings out of the turn and the stern is pushed inside it, the pivot point now being one-third of her length away from the stern (fig. 12). It should be remembered that the pivot point is towards the end of the boat that is leading.

Swivelling propeller Although the effects of turning with one of these are similar to those of a rudder, there will be negligible carry of a boat before answering her helm (due

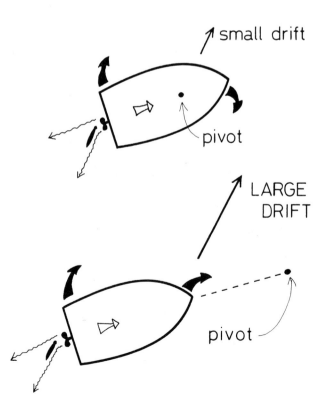

small drift

pivot

LARGE DRIFT

pivot

11 **Drift enlarges the turning radius**

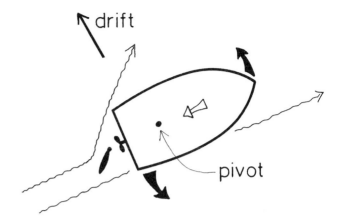

drift

pivot

12 Turning while going astern

to the instant strong slipstream in the required direction), and there will be little drag effect, due to the lack of rudder blade area.

Rudder shape As long as a rudder is large enough and in the right place, its precise shape is of only academic interest to us. However, look at the rudder in fig. 13, a type common on long-keeled sailing craft and excellent for sailing, being a good size and very sturdily hinged to the keel. It is not so good for manoeuvring under power, though, as only a fairly small width of rudder is available in the slipstream of the prop, and even that, due to the section cut away from the leading edge to accommodate the prop, will actually swing out of the slipstream altogether when it is hard over. At slow speeds, the efficiency of a rudder when motoring is entirely dependent on it being in the slipstream of the prop.

13 Deep-keel yacht with a tapered rudder, narrow by the prop

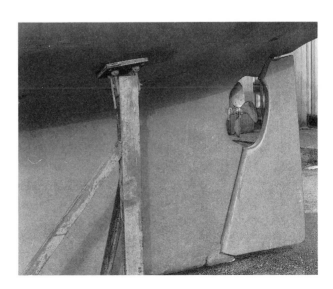

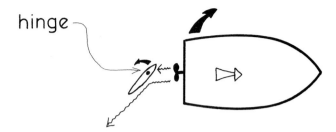

hinge

14 **Balanced rudder**

At high speeds, on the other hand, this very efficiency can make a rudder hard to turn against the flow of water, and very fast boats are often fitted with *balanced rudders*. These are pivoted abaft their leading edges so that a small part of the rudder extends forward of the stock: the moment the rudder is turned slightly the flow of water striking this forward edge helps to push it round (fig. 14).

Propeller Types

As well as the variations in propeller design discussed earlier, there are some specialised types of propeller in common use that have their own handling peculiarities.

Variable pitch propeller As its name implies, this has movable blades that can be twisted in the boss to vary their pitch. The prop itself turns continually in the same direction, with the engine running constantly at its most efficient speed, and the pitch is varied to control the speed of the boat. The faster the boat goes the more easily can the prop grip the water, and the coarser the pitch that can be turned by the engine. Thus a fine pitch can be set for starting off (when inertia is greatest), and the pitch gradually coarsened to increase speed.

Variable pitch is particularly useful on motorsailers as the pitch can be adjusted to the speed of the boat when motor-sailing (see Chapter 8). It is also efficient for trawlers, which can select a fine pitch for towing heavy gear slowly and a coarser pitch for hurrying home, when far less effort is required to push the boat. Such a prop is complex and obviously relatively expensive, but it does obviate the need for a gearbox because the blades can be swivelled right round to convert a right-handed prop into a left-handed one. As it continues to turn clockwise, it will then pull the boat astern (see fig. 10). Neutral is obtained by setting the pitch to zero, so that there will be no drive in either direc-tion. If fitted to a sailing craft, it is usually also possible to turn the blades so that they present the minimum surface area to the direction of travel, thus reducing considerably the drag of the prop when sailing. This is known as *feathering*. Because the prop rotates the same way ahead and astern, paddlewheel effect will always pull the stern in the same direction (fig. 15,16,17,18).

Folding propeller The two blades are hinged loosely at the boss so that water pressure when sailing pushes them back to lie snugly together in line with the shaft. The water resistance is then minimal, as you can see in figs. 19 and 20, and they are commonly employed on sailing yachts to reduce drag when sailing. When the shaft rotates, centrifugal force throws the blades out into their driving position and the boat is pushed along. They are rather inefficient going astern, however, as the thrust of the water tends to fold them up!

Feathering propeller This type is also fitted to sailing yachts to reduce drag when sailing. Generally two-bladed so that it can be aligned with the sternpost, it can be adjusted to feather (some do so automatically) when sailing, and is used with a conventional gearbox. Going astern, it is as efficient as a fixed prop.

Autoprop This recent invention claims the magical ability to take up the most suitable blade pitch for the conditions automatically through special pivoting blades. When starting from rest, the water pressure pushes them into a fine pitch to give maximum grip. As the boat gathers speed the effort required to push her decreases and the blades automatically swing out to steadily increase the pitch, and so their efficiency. On going astern, they swing right round and present their forward faces to the direction of travel, thereby creating a marked increase in efficiency compared with the conventional prop that works back to front when going astern. This improves stopping ability considerably. When motor-sailing (see Chapter 8) this prop sets itself to the most efficient pitch. A price has to be paid for all this, of course: the autoprop is about four times the price of a conventional fixed prop, although actually cheaper than certain self-feathering props.

Propeller Configurations

Not all boats are driven by a single propeller set on the centreline, although this is a very common system. Some are designed with special configurations for certain purposes, while others will be found with a rich variety of weird and wonderful arrangements—often necessitated by

15 **Left-handed variable pitch prop** FULL AHEAD

16 **The same prop** FULL ASTERN **(note finer pitch for less speed)**

17 **The same prop in neutral (note zero pitch: no drive)**

18 **The same prop feathered for sailing**

19 **Folding prop—open**

20 **Folding prop—shut**

structural difficulties in fitting centreline props, but some-times simply because some past owner has had more ingenuity than money! As can be imagined, placing the propeller away from the centreline will have a marked effect on the handling of a boat.

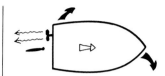

21 **Offset propeller**

Offset propeller

If the prop is not on the hull's centreline it will tend to twist her round all the time (fig. 21). This type of installation is more common on old sailing craft that have been con-verted to auxiliary power, for structural reasons.

It is tempting to believe that fitting a prop in which the paddlewheel effect opposes the offset effect will make the boat run straight—the two cancelling each other out. Unfortunately, because paddlewheel effect varies, they rarely do; and then one can never be certain which way the stern will swing when manoeuvring at slow speed. In practice, an offset prop normally turns outwards—a right-handed prop would be fitted on the starboard side—so that the two effects work in conjunction and the behaviour of the boat is at least predictable.

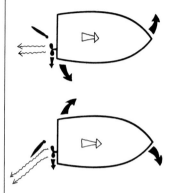

22 **Turning with an offset prop**

Although it may seem that this makes the boat capable only of turning in one direction at slow speeds (when there is little water flow), this is not at all the case, as you can see in fig. 22. The combination of paddlewheel and offset effects with this right-handed prop will assist her in turning to port, but slipstream from the prop will only flow over the rudder when she is steering and turning to starboard.

If the prop is fairly close to the centreline, as in fig. 23, it is very likely that she will actually turn more readily to starboard, if given sufficient blast of slipstream over the rudder. Wherever it is, she can be turned effectively, and predictably, either way with an outward-turning prop—be it right-handed on the starboard quarter or left-handed on the port quarter. Her behaviour when going astern will also be predictable, due to propeller effects again acting in unison.

Offset propeller effect wll also be found with a small boat's outboard clamped on one side of the transom, or with a below-the-hull outdrive system set to one side of the keel. The further from the centreline the propeller is sited, the greater will be the effect.

Twin screws

With two propellers, one set on each side of the centre-line, the same reasoning applies. If both props are outward-turning, considerable predictable side-thrust is obtained from each: the starboard right-handed prop pulling the stern strongly to starboard, and the port left-handed one

23 Offset prop, but close to the centreline

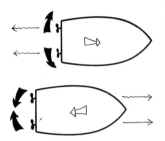

24 Outward turning props, in reverse and ahead gear

pulling it to port, when going ahead. With the props in reverse gear to go astern, they turn inwards and the paddlewheel effect of each one again reinforces its offset effects (see figs. 24 and 25).

When proceeding in a straight line ahead or astern, the side-thrust of each prop is balanced by that of the other and the boat goes straight. When manoeuvring the thrusts can be varied in order to swing the stern as required, one prop even being stopped or run astern if necessary. If the props are inward-turning, side-thrust is both unpredictable and greatly reduced, making the boat much more difficult and unreliable to manoeuvre, both ahead and astern.

If twin variable pitch propellers are fitted, however, there is a good case for installing them as inward-turning. Although the side-thrust from each screw will be both small and unpredictable when going ahead, they will be predictable and at their maximum on going astern—when it is likely to be more important. Because the propellers do not change their direction of rotation when put astern, they will then have the same configuration as conventional outward-turning ones, which do. If each propeller has its own rudder directly behind it (as in fig. 25), manoeuvring ahead with inward-turning props can be improved by using slipstream. With a single rudder on the centreline, such as may be found on a twin-screw motorsailer, the benefits of outward-turning props become even more important.

The reasons for fitting twin screws are usually rather more positive than for fitting a single offset prop. The strong side-thrust obtainable from each independently controllable prop gives greater manoeuvrability than is possible with a single propeller (although see Chapter 2). If all controls and systems are independent for each side, one can be used if the other breaks down. High-speed craft can more efficiently employ two small engines than one large

25 **Twin screws on a modern high-speed lifeboat. The four-bladed equipoise-type props work in undisturbed water clear of the hull. Twin rudders are normally fitted to twin-screw power craft in order to best use the slipstream of each prop. Here they are slightly offset outboard of the props, so that when turning with just the outside prop in use maximum blade area is presented to the slipstream (the rudder being swung in across the prop), thus giving increased turning effect to add to that obtained from the propeller effects**

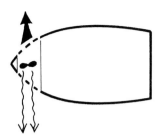

26 Bow thrust pushing bow sideways

one, as installation and weight distribution are more convenient, and smaller props can be turned faster by lighter engines. Twin screws are thus usually encountered on fast boats, or when the requirements of installation and weight distribution preclude the use of a big, heavy single engine (in some large motorsailers, for example).

Wing propeller

This is often fitted to conventional centreline single-screw vessels for emergency propulsion should the main machinery fail. It is usually a small fixed prop set under one quarter and driven by its own auxiliary engine, or else an outboard fixed permanently in some convenient position. It is likely to be difficult to manoeuvre a boat under wing engine only due to the offset effect and considerably reduced power. It is not normally used in conjunction with the main engine, although this may be worth experimenting with if you have one.

Bow thruster

This is a tunnel athwartships through the hull right for'ard below the water, in which there is a propeller that can be controlled to push the bow across one way or the other (fig. 26). Much in use on large ferries and other ships requiring particularly precise and tug-free manoeuvring when berthing, thrusters are becoming increasingly popular with owners of large yachts and motor cruisers.

These yacht types generally protrude below the hull like the leg of an outboard motor.

Summary

Although all these effects may seem to make the driving of a boat under power a complex business, it is important to think of them as allies and not as nuisances. Some of the time, of course, they can make life difficult, but with a little forethought all the subsidiary effects of propulsion and steering systems can—if thoroughly understood—be utilised very much to the benefit of the helmsman trying to wriggle his boat into a small space. How often, for example, have you wished you could swing the back end of your car directly sideways into a tight parking spot!

2 Basic Handling Techniques

Let us now see how we can use the information in Chapter 1 to actually move a boat around in the water, assuming for the time being no wind or current influence. Such basic handling should be second nature before you embark on complex manoeuvring or berthing, as it gives you the knowledge of exactly how she will behave in all circumstances. The knowledge improves with practice, and that is just what you should do with the very basic handling techniques we are going to discuss in this chapter. You should hone your knowledge of the boat until you can gauge within an inch where *all* parts of her will go when you fiddle with throttle or steering. It is of little use putting the stern in the right place if you have only a hazy idea of where the bow will go, and no idea of her overall drift.

To avoid wordiness and complexity when describing the various happenings at the stern of a boat while she is manoeuvring, the phrase *propeller effects* will be used to mean the combined result of paddlewheel effect plus offset effect (where applicable). Turning a boat *against propeller effects* will mean turning in such a direction that they oppose the swing of the stern. Turning her *with propeller effects* will mean turning so that they assist the swing.

The Effects of Hull Shape

We considered in Chapter 1 the effect on turning that the underwater area of a hull will have. The actual form of the hull underwater will also affect virtually all aspects of handling any boat.

A boat with a long keel, presenting great resistance to the water at both bow and stern, will turn less readily than one with a short keel amidships and little depth for'ard and aft. The former will thus hold a straight course more easily, due to her disinclination to turn. The short-keeled craft will turn very quickly when you want her to, but also when you do not want her to; e.g. the slightest quiver in the rudder when starting a turn, which is easily over-corrected to produce a continual yawing effect. This can be a problem in certain conditions, as we will see in later chapters. It also causes propeller effects to swing the stern more quickly than they will in a long-keeled boat.

Directional stability (the tendency to hold a straight course) is also better when the draft of a boat is deeper aft. If she swings off course, the deep stern will act like a rudder or weathervane and the flow of water past it will force her back on course. If she is deeper for'ard the flow of water will force the bow to continue its swing, and such a boat will be extremely difficult to steer in a straight line.

In fig. 27 you can see a modern fin-keeled yacht alongside a more traditional long-keel type. Note that the long keel is cut away for'ard, partly to ensure the directional stability of depth aft, but also to help her turn. If a keel this deep was straight and continued all the way to the bow, her directional stability would be so great that she would hardly turn at all! Displacement power boats, with considerably less depth of keel than this, will have a more even distribution of draft, although the greatest depth will still be aft (fig. 28).

27 Long-keel and fin-and-spade hulls

28 The antifouling extends above the waterline at the bow

Planing boats at rest are generally deeper for'ard than aft, due to the trim requirements when planing, and this can give rise to steering difficulties at low speeds, when they are displacing water, not planing over it. These are sometimes resolved by fitting skegs under the hull at the stern, as in fig. 29 and also the very deep skeg under the stern of the lifeboat in fig. 25. Without such skegs planing boats are often easier to steer astern than ahead when they are not on the plane.

The deeper the Vee of a planing boat's bottom, the more likely she is to have sufficient depth aft to give reasonable directional stability without the need for skegs. Compare the shapes of the sterns in figs. 29 and 32.

Sailing boats with centreboards or leeboards will turn under power more readily (and drift less) with their boards lowered, although directional stability will be reduced. They will then have the hull shape of a fin-keel yacht. The Thames Sailing Barges (fig. 30) had leeboards on their flat-bottomed hulls; the one on the outside of the turn should be used, so that drift presses it in against the side rather than pulling on its fastenings. Multihulls, particularly catamarans, also turn reluctantly, due to the drag of the extra hulls being hauled round. They turn best if they have a deep rocker to the keel, thus giving them more depth amidships and less at the ends.

The disparate hull shapes of displacement and planing boats cause them to behave quite differently when turning at speed. The former lean out of turns due to centrifugal force on their above-water hulls, while the latter lean into them due to the shape of their bilges. This is particularly noticeable with a deep-Vee hull because of the steep rise of floor, which she leans down on. This type of hull, if taken to an extreme, can be somewhat precarious when running straight, due to a tendency to fall over onto one bilge!

29 **Planing bottom with small rudders, and skegs which also protect the shafts and props somewhat**

30 **Leeboard raised completely**

The Importance of Trim

The trim of a vessel is the attitude in which she sits in the water as seen in a fore-and-aft line. Altering the trim will change the underwater form and clearly this will affect performance and handling.

Trim and propulsion

A propeller shaft is designed to make a certain angle with the waterline for the prop to work at its best. If a boat is trimmed down too much by the stern, the propeller will waste power trying to push the boat up into the air. If she is trimmed too much by the bow, however, not only might the prop try to drive her down towards the seabed, but it will also be working too close to the surface (assuming this trim has lifted the stern). This will reduce its thrust and also make it prone to *ventilating*—sucking air around the blades and thus losing its grip on the water. The same problems can also be caused by the whole boat sitting too high in the water. Ventilation is most likely with outboards and outdrives that work close to the surface all the time, and is prevented by means of flat plates fastened to the units immediately above the props (fig. 31). These plates reduce the likelihood of air being sucked down from the surface.

Cavitation is rather different from ventilation, although the two are often confused. It occurs when a prop loses pressure on the front of its blades, causing the water to boil at the back of them and form bubbles of vapour which give no more grip to the prop than air. As well as loss of drive, cavitation can also cause bits of the metal to break

31 **Anti-ventilation plate over the propeller**

off. A cavitating prop gives off a loud banging roar, and is most usually experienced on sudden acceleration in a high-speed craft; also with small auxiliary yacht props crashing around in a head sea. It is caused by excessive loading on the prop.

The angle between the leg of an outboard or outdrive and the transom is usually adjustable, partly to allow for differently angled transoms, and partly to allow for or correct the trim of planing boats. This adjustment can often be made by operating a control in the wheelhouse, although small outboards are adjusted by a large retaining pin in one of a selection of holes in the transom bracket. This bracket, and the anti-cavitation plate (as it is usually wrongly called), can both be seen clearly on the outboard in fig. 31. Under the plate is a miniature rudder that can be set so as to counteract the slight paddlewheel effect of this type of prop.

Trim of planing craft

When actually planing, fore-and-aft trim is affected not only by weight distribution but also by speed and the sea conditions. Such boats are generally designed to plane with their bows up a little, to prevent nose-diving into waves. To bring the bow down and improve the trim in calm water they are often fitted with adjustable trim-tabs at the bottom of each side of the transom: their angle can be altered so that the water pressure acting on them will force the stern up and level out the trim. They can also be used individually to push up one side of a deep-Vee boat if she falls over (fig. 32). Altering the angle of outboard or outdrive can also adjust the trim.

32 **Trim tabs on lower edge of transom, activated by hydraulic rams**

Trim and steering

The effect on steering of altering the trim should be apparent from the earlier section on hull shape. If a boat is down by the head, she can become almost impossible to steer. If she is listed heavily to one side her steering will also be affected, due to her natural inclination to list when turning: she will turn more readily in the direction that would cause her to list the way she already does. A displacement boat will have a tendency to turn away from the side to which she is listed and be reluctant to turn towards it, while a planing boat will tend to turn towards her list, and be reluctant to turn away from it. A lot of people standing for'ard or on one side of a small boat could induce sufficient list or alteration in trim to affect the steering in these ways.

Moving off Ahead

This may seem a very simple operation, but the propeller effects explained in Chapter 1 can easily add a little spice to it. There are three important things you must have quite clear in your mind before you go ahead, whether stopped or already moving: how much delay there will be from propeller slip before the boat responds; how rapidly she will then accelerate; and how the stern will swing with prop effects. With a hydraulically operated gearbox there may also be a delay before the prop even begins to turn, when starting from rest.

In order to be able to judge these things accurately, it is most important that you be aware at all times of your boat's precise movement in relation to the water. From the handling viewpoint there are two ways in which a boat can move: in relation to the water, and in relation to the ground. When judging the approach to a berth, or assessing the effects of wind and current, the latter is most important and it will be explained in the next two chapters. The movement *through the water*, however, is what affects propeller and rudder, and this must be constantly checked by looking over the side.

You must also know at all times the angle of your rudder or swivelling prop. If this is not easily visible from the wheel, a helm indicator should be fitted where it can be readily seen.

Moving off Astern

There are some important differences from moving off ahead. The blunter shape of the average stern magnifies propeller slip delay and paddlewheel effect, and with the slipstream flowing forward a rudder will not work until some speed through the water has built up. This may take some time, as gearboxes usually transmit a good deal less power astern than they do ahead.

Thus, unless the boat can be kept straight by directing the thrust of a swivelling prop, or adjusting throttles to balance the opposing side-thrusts of twin screws, she will slowly move off astern in an arc, the direction and extent of which depends on her propeller effects and hull shape. It will not be possible to straighten her until she has sufficient speed through the water to activate her rudder. Even then it may be necessary to stop the propeller, and hence its effects if they are strong, to enable the rudder to straighten her without having to build up excessive speed.

It is possible to overcome this to a certain extent by first giving her a brief kick ahead with the rudder over, to swing the stern the opposite way. She will still curve astern in the same arc eventually, but it will be in a different place. In fig. 33 you can see a boat with a single right-handed prop using this technique to negotiate the corner of a jetty. If she had not built up sufficient speed by position 3 to give the rudder steerage, another kick ahead as in position 1 would swing her stern clear of the wall.

It is essential that these kicks ahead are short and sharp—

33 Backing round a corner

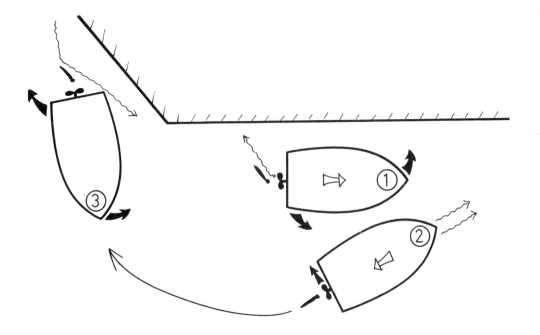

just sufficient power to bring slipstream effect into play without generating thrust ahead—or you will simply shunt back and forth in the same spot. This may happen anyway if you try this with a variable pitch prop, as the paddlewheel effect ahead will oppose the slipstream effect.

If you go too fast astern in a bid to get the rudder working, you could find it difficult to control as it will be pivoting at the wrong end. Instead of trying to straighten it, the water flow will attempt to push it hard over with some force; even wrench it from the helmsman's grip violently enough to damage the steering gear, as well as create havoc with the manoeuvre he is carrying out. A firm hand is needed, and speed kept to the minimum consistent with steering control. If the rudder does take charge, use the slipstream from a hard kick ahead to straighten up both rudder and boat.

With twin screws the rudders are best left amidships while moving astern (a sternboard) and the direction controlled by varying the throttles. To begin with you may have to keep swinging her back into line by stopping one prop, or even kicking it ahead, but with practice you will soon develop the knack of keeping her quite straight with constant slight adjustment of the throttles. If you want her to curve one way, simply slow down the prop on the inside of the curve or speed up the outer one; the increased sidethrust of the outside prop will pull her stern round. The tightness of the curve can be varied with the throttles as required, and experience should enable you to slalom wherever you wish. You should try to anticipate the beginning of a swing and correct it with just a touch of throttle adjustment bfore the stern actually starts moving noticeably.

Stopping the Boat

This takes time, whatever the propulsion and steering system, during which a heavy boat moving at speed could cover a fair distance. If she happens to arrive at a concrete wall or a flimsy yacht during this period, the result is likely to upset your insurance company. The greater the speed and the heavier the boat, the more her momentum and the longer she will take to stop; although this will be affected by the design of the hull and propeller, and the power transmitted astern by the gearbox. Most variations on this general rule occur with auxiliary yachts, whose often inefficient propellers and low-powered engines can cause them to take far longer to stop than their hulls and speeds might indicate. (Note the comment in Chapter 1 on folding props.)

Besides taking a long time to stop, even when going full astern, certain boats will sheer wildly to one side during the process (especially those with short keels), due to the exaggerated propeller effects caused by going astern while the boat is moving ahead. This will occur to varying extents with all configurations other than swivelling propellers or twin screws, both of which can be controlled to hold the boat straight while she slows down, as explained above. It is particularly important to know your boat's behaviour on going full astern to stop in an emergency, as a strong sheer in the wrong direction might well make things worse. It may be that some other course of action—perhaps full power ahead using slipstream to assist a tight turn—could give you a better chance of extricating yourself.

Beware also the sudden sheer that you can get when shifting into neutral, if prop effects cause a boat to constantly require a little rudder angle in order to run straight. This is particularly noticeable with an outward-turning offset prop. The moment the prop effects cease a boat will swing according to how the rudder is set. This can be cured by immediately straightening the rudder on going into neutral.

Most of the time you will not be stopping to avert an emergency, but simply to berth alongside or pick up a buoy. It is just as important to know the result of prop effects in these situations, or the boat will not end up where you want her. More positively, you can use them in order to put her where you want (see later chapters).

When going astern from ahead (or vice versa), whatever the propulsion system you should always allow the gearbox a brief pause in neutral before engaging the next gear, to give all the cogs a little time to settle. You should also engage the gear firmly and solidly so that the clutch does not slip and wear. Never flick a manual lever into gear and let it bounce around: this is akin to riding the clutch of a car, and worse. Your gearbox will not last long if you do this.

Turning at Low Speed

It is essential to appreciate that a boat with a rudder can best be turned at low speeds by driving a powerful flow of water from the propeller across the rudder: the slow water flow past the boat will produce very sluggish steering. If this burst of slipstream is strong but short, the boat can be turned before the propeller thrust starts her moving ahead. A tight turn can thus be made by using a succession of short, sharp bursts of power, maximising the turning effect of the slipstream while minimising forward movement.

Turning Short

The simplest system is the swivelling prop, which will produce a tight turn at any speed simply by swivelling hard round. An even tighter turn may be made by going astern halfway through the manoeuvre and reversing the angle of the prop so as to pull the stern hard round in the required direction and also astern a little before coming ahead again (fig. 34). The stages of the turn are shown separately here for clarity (and in the next few illustrations), although in reality it would be made virtually on the spot. It should not be necessary to consider paddlewheel effect, which for a small prop will be negligible in comparison with the turning moment of the angled slipstream.

Twin screws are also easily turned short, simply by stopping or reversing the prop on the inside of the turn. With the outside prop going ahead and the inside one astern, she will turn right round on the spot without any need to touch the rudders. However, this is not the most efficient way to turn a twin-screw boat short as it takes a long time, and does not generate sufficient turning power to swing her into the wind. She will turn more rapidly and with greater power if you first go ahead on the outer screw with the inner one stopped, then stop it and go astern on the inner, all the time allowing the boat to move through the water either ahead or astern as required (fig. 35).

A single-screw boat with a rudder can, surprisingly perhaps, be turned more tightly than twin screws, being capable of a three-point turn quite literally on the spot. In fig. 36 you can see a boat with a right-handed prop making one. The secret is to make the initial turn against the propeller effects, giving a brief hard kick ahead to swing her with the slipstream over a fully angled rudder. As soon as

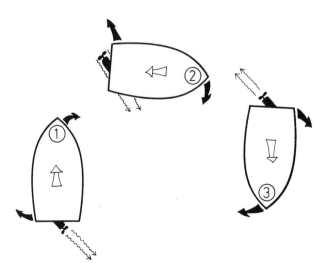

34 **Tight turn with a swivelling prop**

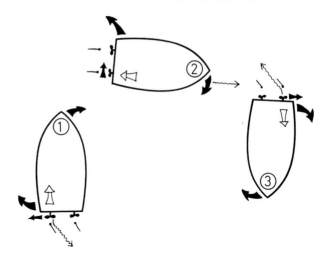

35 Tight turn with twin screws

the stern begins to swing, put her full astern and allow the increased prop effects in astern gear to continue pulling her stern round; there is no need to alter the position of the rudder as it will only have effect when the prop is going ahead. Then go ahead again as before, and repeat the whole cycle as often as necessary. As long as you never allow the boat to actually gather any way ahead or astern, simply using prop effects or slipstream to swing the stern sideways each time, she will turn on the spot quickly and powerfully. The more nearly stopped the boat is to begin with, the tighter will be the turn.

An outward-turning offset prop should also be turned in this way, in order to utilise the considerable prop effects when going astern. If, however, it is offset so far that its slipstream by-passes the rudder, the initial turn may have to be made with sufficient way on to activate the rudder.

36 Single-screw tight turn

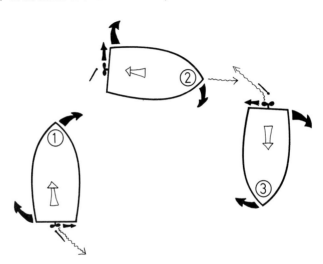

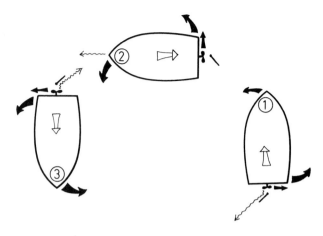

A variable pitch propeller, revolving the same way for ahead and astern, should be initially turned with slipstream assisted by paddlewheel effect as this will not change on going astern. You will have beneficial paddlewheel effect during all stages of the manoeuvre (fig. 37).

Manoeuvring with Bow Thrust

In its simplest role a bow thruster can be used to push the bow whichever way is required, for turning tightly. In this role it reinforces the swing imparted to the stern by rudder and/or propeller effects. In addition, if it is used in opposition to the swing of the stern the boat can be made to move bodily sideways, as in fig. 38. This trick can also be employed when going astern, in conjunction with the propeller effects (fig. 39). The overall movement of the boat will be as shown by the thin arrows, due to the combination of sideways movement and ahead or astern thrust. Main propulsion can thus be juggled to obtain the precise direction wanted.

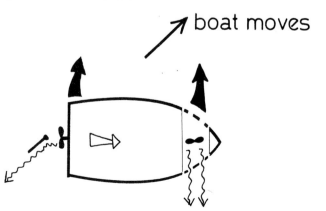

38 **Bow thrust with ahead power**

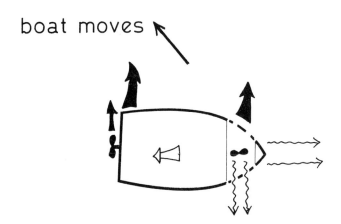

39 Bow thrust in astern gear

Summary

It is not possible, nor advisable, to give a detailed description of how to carry out every type of manoeuvre in every type of craft in all circumstances. To attempt to do so would make this book far too big, and even then most readers would, within a week, come across a situation that had not been described. The secret of good boat handling under power is to thoroughly understand the basic forces produced by a propulsion unit, a steering system, and a boat's hull; and then to learn how to judge the way these forces interact, and assess and anticipate the result of this interaction on the movement of a particular boat in the circumstances.

When faced with an unusual configuration, say of propulsion and steering on a boat, you must take time to carefully consider how all the forces produced by the components of the system will interact. If, for example, a propeller is offset, you should not simply say to yourself: 'Propeller is offset to starboard, so boat will turn more easily to port.' You must appreciate and weigh up all the other factors involved, as discussed in these first two chapters. Even if in the end only experiment wll tell exactly how a boat will behave, it is important that you know why she does what she does, or you will never be able to assess properly how external factors such as wind or current, spring lines and so on (to be discussed in later chapters) will affect her. In the Appendix you will find details of some less commonly encountered propulsion and steering systems.

3 Manoeuvring in Wind and Stream

Before we can learn to adjust our basic handling techniques in order to allow for—and exploit—the effects of wind and stream, it is essential to understand the crucial difference between the two. The effect that the wind has on a boat is quite different from that exerted by moving water, and much poor boat handling stems from an inability to appreciate this.

The Effect of a Stream

The stream or current is, in effect, a moving sheet of water (rather like a conveyor belt) that carries floating objects, such as a boat, bodily in the direction and at the speed it is moving. It does not affect her attitude, any more than a conveyor belt affects the position of a box sitting on it. Both simply move the object over the ground, so that it appears to go forwards, backwards or sideways, depending on the way in which it sits on the belt.

The movement over the ground of a boat under the influence of a stream is therefore not affected in the slightest by her shape or size, nor her speed or course. A 500,000 ton oil tanker travelling at 16 knots will be moved over the ground by a stream exactly the same distance and in exactly the same direction as a floating log. The overall movement of the two will be quite different since the ship is also propelled by her engines, but the part of each movement that is caused by the stream will be identical.

As a stream moves a boat *over the ground* only (it cannot move her in relation to the water), it has no direct effect whatever on the behaviour of propulsion and steering systems, which are affected only by movement of the boat through the water.

Distinctions between the terms 'stream' and 'current' are irrelevant: whether moving water is encountered in a river or at sea, as a result of tides or not, makes no difference. However, at times it is useful to realize that the speed of flow is not always uniform, particularly near shore. This difference can sometimes be put to good use, as when turning round.

The Effect of Wind

Wind moves a boat *through the water*, making its influence on her rather more complex and numerous than the single effect of a stream. Every single effect that wind has on a boat stems from one basic fact: the more difficult she is to move through the water, the less the wind will move her. This may seem obvious, but if you keep it in mind as we discuss the variety of behaviour that results from it, you will find all the effects of wind considerably simpler to understand and visualise.

When a wind blows against the parts of a boat that are above water and thus exposed to it—hull sides, super-structure, masts, rigging, etc—its pressure causes the boat to move in the same direction as the wind. This drifting movement, however, is opposed by the resistance of the water to those parts of the boat immersed in it, i.e. the underwater part of the hull, the rudder and sterngear, and anything else attached to the boat that is under the water.

If there was no resistance to the movement of the boat, the wind would simply blow her along. The overall resist-ance of the water, however, can very roughly be considered to slow her down ten-fold: i.e. approximately 20 knots of wind would be needed to move her at the 2 knots that 2 knots of stream would. This is no more than an extremely general guide: the precise rate will vary considerably with the windage and water resistance of the individual boat. It should be apparent that the boat on the left in fig. 40 will drift a good deal faster than the one on the right.

This may seem an extreme example, but compare the small motor cruiser in fig. 41 with the open Shetland-type boat in fig. 42 (part of whose keel is hidden in the mud). Both of these boats would, however, if they were as sym-metrical as shown in fig. 40, simply drift bodily through the water, directly downwind.

Boats, however, are rarely symmetrical. One end will have more windage than the other, and one end will have more underwater body than the other. Thus the pressure of wind will be greater at one end of the boat than the other, and so will the water resistance. The effect of this is that the wind will swing the boat rather like a weathervane,

40 Windage above water enhances drift; deep draft slows it

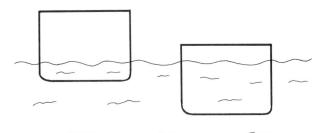

41 **Small cruiser with a
long straight keel**

42 **Double-ended
Shetland boat with rocker
bottom**

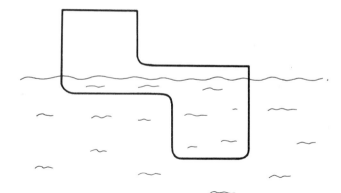

43 Wind will push the taller end off to leeward, like a weathervane

the end with more windage drifting more than the other, and the end with most water resistance drifting less. You can visualise what would happen to the rather nasty-looking object in fig. 43.

In practice windage and water resistance are distributed somewhat less evenly than this. To assess the effect of wind on a boat we must average out her windage to see roughly where the bulk of it lies, and thus where the wind will appear to push on her; and do the same with the underwater hull area to see where the maximum water resistance will be felt. The former position is known as the *Centre of Effort* (of the wind), and the latter as the *Centre of Lateral Resistance* (to movement through the water). Under the influence of wind the CE of the boat will blow away faster than the CLR, just as the larger tail of a weathervane blows away downwind.

It should be apparent that the head of the fishing boat in fig. 44 will be blown off quite rapidly to leeward, due to her high bow and for'ard wheelhouse, and the deep draft at the stern, and you can see an example of this quite

44 Typical high forward windage of small fishing boats

45 Most of the windage is forward

common type in fig. 45. Sailing yachts, with bows higher than their sterns and the windage of mast and rigging for'ard, behave similarly, and the for'ard windage of a fairly typical small yacht can be seen in fig. 46. In fact, most boats under power tend to have their Centres of Effort ahead of their Centres of Lateral Resistance, and so their bows blow off the wind, to varying degrees.

A sailing vessel with leeboards or centreboard can move her CLR by adjusting the position of the board. The Thames Barge in the photo would have her bows blown off least if she lowered her leeward leeboard so that it swung down and forward as far as possible, so shifting her CLR forward. She would also drift considerably less than with it hauled up as in the photo.

As a boat blows round, however, so her angle to the wind progressively changes, altering the area of superstructure presented to the wind, and the shape of the underwater body as presented to the water along the line of her overall drift. The result is that there comes a point at which the Centre of Effort lies directly downwind of the Centre of Lateral Resistance, whereupon the turning effect disappears. The boat will then maintain this position in relation to the wind and simply drift bodily thereafter.

46 A very different type, again with her windage forward

This stable position is generally roughly beam-on to the wind for the average motorboat. Craft with considerable windage for'ard and deep draft aft—sailing vessels, displacement boats with for'ard wheelhouses, etc—will lie further off the wind. Boats with large aft superstructures and maximum draft for'ard, such as planing boats with huge after sun lounges and suchlike, will lie with their bows closer to the wind (see fig. 47); as probably would the catamaran in fig. 48 whose mast and rigging is much further aft than usual.

The weight (displacement) of a boat will not affect her final rate of drift, but it will affect the time it takes her to accelerate up to it. The great inertia of a heavy boat will cause her to resist the pressure of the wind for much longer than will a light one, so it will take the wind some time to build up her rate of drift to its natural maximum. It also takes a lot more effort to stop the drift of a heavy boat than it does to stop a light one: again due to her greater inertia. These are important points to consider when berthing with an onshore wind.

The effect of wind on a boat, then, is to swing her round until she attains equilibrium (wind pressure balancing water resistance), and to push her through the water in this attitude at a speed very roughly one-tenth of the wind speed; precise effects varying with the design of the boat. There will also be a component of drift over the ground, depending on the movement of the water. If there is no water movement, drift over the ground will equal drift through the water.

47 Despite the flared bow, there is more windage from the superstructure aft

**48 Low bows and most
of the windage aft**

Assessing Drift

Wind-driven drift through the water can be easily estimated for a boat motoring on a steady course by noting the difference in angle between her wake and her course steered (heading), as in fig. 49. When manoeuvring in restricted waters, however, constant heading changes make this unreliable, and general observation of the boat's movement through the water must be relied upon, taking into account that caused by propulsion and steering.

Overall drift *over the ground*, be it caused by wind, stream or both, must be assessed by observing the boat's movement in relation to some object that is on shore or fixed to the seabed. This is best done by means of *transits*, simply a pair of fixed objects kept in line. In fig. 50 you can see a boat in line with a church and a tree on shore. It should be apparent that so long as those objects are kept in line the boat must be somewhere on an extension of that line. You can see what happens if the boat moves to either side of the line: the two marks move apart, the rear one appearing to move the same way as the boat. Very little movement of the line is necessary to make the transit open up. By setting up transits like this in various directions, you can keep a very accurate check on the real movement of the boat over the ground, whether ahead, astern or sideways. Anything can be used as long as it is not moving: buoys, flagstaffs, beacons, cranes, lamp-posts, corners of buildings, headlands and so on. They do not even need to be in line: all you want to know is how the rear one is moving in relation to the front one, which reflects how you are moving over the ground.

You can even set up transits with only one fixed object, by observing its movement against some part of the boat— mast, stanchion, corner of the wheelhouse or whatever. As long as the boat is on a steady course and the position of your eye remains fixed in relation to the marker on the boat,

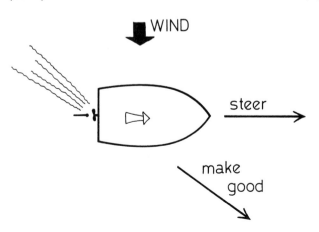

49 **Wind pushing sideways alters the course actually achieved**

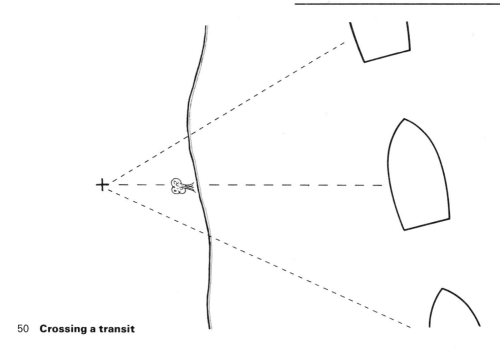

50 **Crossing a transit**

51 **Checking movement in relation to the shore**

the movement of that bit of boat against the shore mark will indicate your movement over the ground. Note that in this instance it is the object nearer the eye that reflects the boat's movement over the ground (fig. 51).

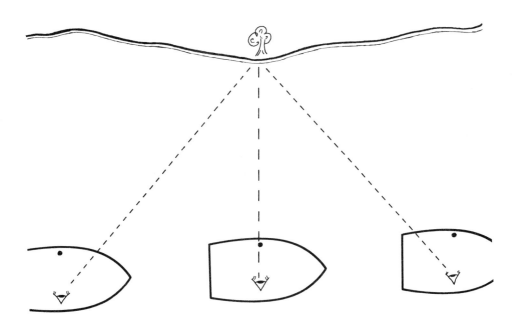

Continually checking movement over the ground by means of transits is a lot less difficult than it sounds, which is just as well as it is most important to be able to do this when manoeuvring towards a berth or otherwise in restricted waters. Whatever the boat may be doing through the water, it is her movement over the ground that gets her from place to place. If there is a particular spot you want to get to—say a mooring buoy or a berth—you must use these transits to check that the boat's overall movement is towards them. If you want to avoid something—shallows, harbour wall, moored boat—you must use them to ensure that your track is not actually towards the hazard. The boat may be on an apparently safe heading, yet be drifting into danger.

In fig. 52 you can see the eye lining up some rigging with a church steeple ashore. The movement of this shroud will not only show the boat's movement over the ground, but also in relation to the sailing yacht standing towards you from the shore, and the large pilot launch moored on the left of the picture. If the shroud remains in line with either of these, it denotes that they are on a steady bearing and you will collide with them. Either tidal drift may be setting you sideways or your two courses are converging.

52 **Lining up fixed rigging to check changes in bearings**

Handling in Streams

The most important point to appreciate about a stream is that it does not move in relation to the boat. In order to control the boat you have to propel her through the water, particularly if you want the rudder to have any effect. If you do this in the same direction as the stream is running, you will move over the ground at the *sum* of the boat's speed through the water and the speed of the water over the ground—which could be far too fast for both the nerves and the brain in restricted waters. If you then wish to stop the boat in relation to the ground, alongside a quay perhaps, you will need to motor astern at the same speed as the stream is running, and against it. With a fast stream and a low-powered auxiliary yacht this may be physically impossible. In almost any stream a boat with uncontrollable propeller effects will sheer sufficiently during the stopping process to end up across the stream, in which position she will have no means whatever of moving against it and off she will go sideways at the speed of the stream, causing acute embarrassment to everyone.

If you motor into the stream, however, all is quite different as your speed over the ground will be the *difference* between your speed and that of the stream. You will find it very easy to control your movement over the ground simply by varying propeller thrust, and movements can be done more slowly. At full ahead you will move forward over the ground at however much faster you are travellling than the stream. If you go ahead through the water at the same speed as the stream, you will remain stationary in relation to the ground. In a strong stream you will be able to motor ahead under perfect control at a slower speed than the stream and actually proceed astern over the ground. It is not hard to visualise the sort of control this gives, especially when you appreciate that slight adjustment of steering and throttle will enable you to crab sideways across the stream at whatever rate and in the direction you wish.

Controlling speed and direction over the ground when motoring across a stream is done in exactly the same way, transits being utilised in all cases for determining your movement. Only when stemming the stream (motoring straight into it) will you have the control to move ahead, astern or remain stopped over the ground. Because of this, all manoeuvring in restricted waters should be done stemming the stream if at all possible.

Clearly, in order to be able to do this you must know the speed and direction of the stream before you get there, or you could find yourself careering downstream into a corner and out of control before you realise what is happening. The general rate and direction of a tidal stream or current

53 **Stream direction indicated by a buoy**

54 **The deeper tug is lying to the stream and beam-on to the wind, whereas the pilot boats behind are affected more by the wind**

in an area can be found from almanac or pilot book, but in restricted waters obstructions can cause localized variations that must be assessed on the spot. This can be done by observing the flow past fixed objects such as buoys, moored boats, piles, rocks and suchlike. In fig. 53 you can see the stream running past a buoy, almost building a bow-wave against the upstream side (a very strong stream would do so, and cause the buoy to heel over noticeably away from it). Moored and anchored boats will lie back from their moorings in the direction the stream is running, unless affected by strong winds, and observing them is an excellent way of determining the direction of a stream from a distance (see the tug and the pilot boats in fig. 54).

The other way to assess the stream in advance is from its likely behaviour as it rounds bends, follows channels and negotiates obstructions. A stream is a stream, whether it runs through a harbour or down a mountain, and it has two main characteristics that are of importance to us. The first is that it always takes the easiest route past obstacles: and the second is that its flow in terms of the *quantity* of water moved per minute remains constant however narrow the gap it is forced to pass through.

The easiest route past a series of obstacles can be seen quite clearly in fig. 55. By and large, streams flow more strongly through narrows, round the outsides of bends and down the middle of a channel. They are weaker on the insides of bends and the edges of channels, and generally quite slack in deep bays, where back-eddies can sometimes be found. They do, however, tend to flow into shallow bays, sometimes squirting out rather rapidly at the other end at right angles to the main set. They often set at an angle across corners and shallow banks, seeking a short-cut to the next deep channel.

It would seem that our neat 'conveyor belt' has spawned some complications. Nothing here, however, alters any-

55 How streams may be altered by the shape of the land

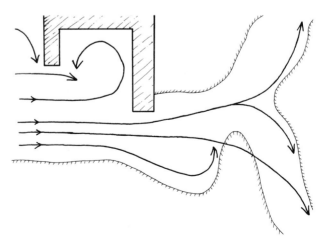

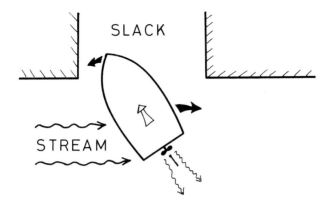

56 Turning out of the stream

thing that has been said about the behaviour of boats in streams. What such variation of stream flow means is that it can be very easy to think you will be stemming a stream on arrival at a berth, then discover—too late—that you are in a back-eddy coming at your stern. Equally, a sudden cross-stream entering or leaving a bay or side channel could sweep you into trouble if you are not aware of its likelihood. So you must think carefully about the probable behaviour of streams when manoeuvring in obstructed waters.

Mostly, however much the stream may vary, it simply carries the boat wherever it happens to be going at the time. If, however, you have to pass a spot where the stream is sharply and suddenly cut off, or reversed, you could find your bow in one stream and stern in another. This can happen when crossing a *tideline* (the junction of two differ-ent streams, or one and a back-eddy—usually marked by a line of scum or a change in wave pattern), or when entering or leaving a lock or dock with a strong cross-stream outside. In rivers, the stream is often much stronger a few feet out from shore, and it can catch the end of the boat.

If you cross a tideline you will suddenly feel the boat swing round as the bow is instantly carried in the direction of the new stream. She will soon straighten, but this must be watched for in tight corners. Entering a dock from a cross-stream is a tight corner, and you could easily be swung onto the wall as the bow suddenly comes out of the stream and into slack water. Have a look at fig. 56.

To hold up against the stream you will be crabbing towards the gap as shown. If you hold this course the bow will swing hard into the port wall as it hits the slack water, and the stream pushing on the stern will swing it into the starboard wall. To avoid both happening you should aim to put your bow into the middle of the entrance, then the moment you feel it enter the slack water give a hard burst of slipstream to swing the stern to port away from the corner. This must be rapidly and steadily reduced as more of the boat enters the slack water so as to avoid swinging the stern right across to the far wall.

To come out of such a place, you should keep close to the upstream wall so that as your bow enters the stream you have room to swing the stern away and power up into it. The faster you come out, the less time you will spend half in and half out of the stream.

Handling in Wind

Coping with the bodily drift from wind is just the same as allowing for stream, bearing in mind its much weaker effect. Although wind eddies will be found in harbours, especially around tall buildings, they will not cause the same problems as stream eddies and variations. Very strong squalls roaring out through gaps must be watched for, however, particularly when handling light planing boats that can be quickly accelerated by the wind.

The effect of wind on the attitude of a boat calls for rather more detailed consideration. From what has been said in an earlier section you will appreciate that if the boat is closer to the wind than her natural position of equilibrium, the wind will blow her bow off downwind—sometimes quite rapidly—until she reaches such position. If she is already further off the wind than that position, the wind will blow her stern round until she reaches it. Generally, wind coming from for'ard of the beam will blow the bow to leeward, while wind abaft the beam will blow the stern to leeward, depending on the type of boat.

These effects will have to be corrected for by using propulsion and steering, strong slipstream often being required to get a boat's head up into the wind, particularly if she has much windage for'ard or little power—both common in auxiliary yachts which can be difficult to keep up into the wind when it is strong. The old smack in fig. 57 would have great difficulty in getting her head round into a strong wind with all those spars and rigging for'ard, especially as she probably has little power and a long keel. If propeller effects work against her turn towards the wind (she will probably have an offset prop some distance from the rudder), it will very likely be virtually impossible to get her round in a blow.

When going astern a boat's pivot point moves aft and this has a strange effect on her behaviour in a breeze. The pivot point moves aft, to a position one-third of her length from the stern. This causes the wind on her bow to act on a longer turning lever, thus increasing its effect. The result is that in strong winds the stern—quite regardless of prop effects, the position of the rudder, or anything else—climbs inexorably towards the wind, and continues to do so, even

57 **Traditional rigging carries a penalty of greater windage**

against the full opposite turning effect of twin screws, until it is pointing directly upwind. As long as astern power is continued, she will then back directly into the wind, the only thing able to oppose it in a strong wind being a bow thruster. We shall refer to this throughout the book as 'the draw of the wind'.

This is a quite dominant feature of handling boats under power in any strength of wind, and it can often make close-quarter manoeuvring rather difficult. However, its very strength and certainty provides a convenient and reliable escape route should things go wrong. If you find her head blowing rapidly off towards a jetty or moored boat and there is insufficient room to blast round into the wind with slipstream, going full astern—whatever the attitude of the

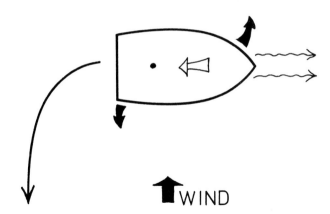

58 Backing in a cross-wind

WIND

boat at the time—will nearly always pull you out of trouble straight astern and upwind.

Although this effect is experienced with all boats, it will clearly be stronger with a single-screw boat whose prop effects are reinforcing it than with a twin-screw boat working hard to pull her stern the other way. It will also be stronger in a boat that naturally lies bow downwind (see fig. 58).

Using Wind and Stream

It is not necessary, however, to constantly do battle with wind, stream and propulsion system all together. Wind and stream can often be employed alone to drift the boat into a certain position or angle, after which propulsion can then be used to move her in a different direction if desired. Fig. 59 shows a nice example where a boat, instead of trying to turn hard round a couple of tight bends, simply stops and allows the stream to carry her past an obstruction, after which she can proceed again under power. This avoids all the swinging and drifting that would occur if she tried to turn hard round both bends, and gives precise control over her positioning.

With a stream on one bow, occasional touches ahead on the engine can cause the boat to move sideways in a very calm and controlled manner, and this is a technique that can be used most effectively for edging across into a tight berth (fig. 60).

Where a stream is running hard through a narrow gap or harbour entrance, it can often be advisable to enter stern first. You can then adjust speed and attitude against the stream so that it actually carries you astern through the gap, while your propulsion and steering going ahead against the stream give you complete control of the boat.

Turning tightly in a small space can often be assisted by

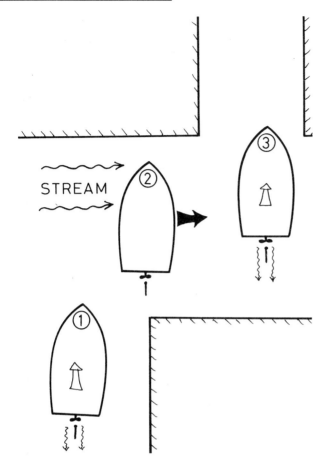

STREAM

59 **Using the stream to move sideways without power or turning**

drawing the stern up into the wind, or hindered by having the wind blow against the bow. It is important to take the direction of the wind into account when turning short as described in Chapter 2, arranging the turn so that the sternboard is towards the wind rather than away from it.

If a bow thruster is used to counteract the draw of the wind on the stern, the result will be to move bodily sideways upwind, the thruster pushing the bow up and the wind drawing the stern up. If this takes her too far upwind, both thruster and propeller should be stopped and boat simply allowed to drift back downwind again.

Summary

It is very easy when under the influence of strong winds or stream to be carried into an inextricable position, and constant vigilance is necessary under such circumstances.

If you need to buy time (to survey a berth perhaps), or you get into bother, remember the benefits of stemming the stream and drawing astern into the wind. It is generally a mistake to try and hold a boat head-to-wind (particularly if she has high windage for'ard), as the slightest deviation off course will bring it onto one bow and cause her to pay off rapidly.

60 Using power and the stream on one bow to edge sideways

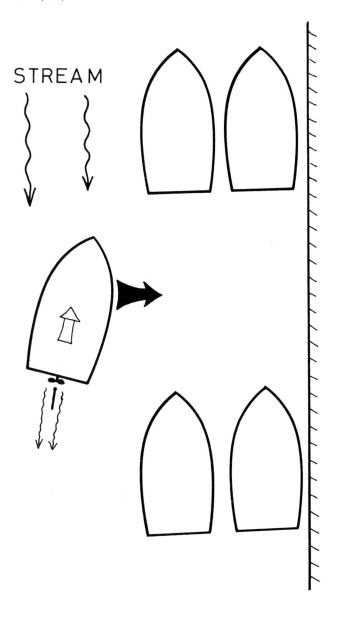

STREAM

4 Berthing Alongside

If you have thoroughly understood everything so far discussed, you should be able to work all this out for yourself. However, that is something of a counsel of perfection, so let us consider how one goes about getting a boat alongside.

The aim should be to have her stopped, in relation to the ground, in precisely the place you want her to lie: close enough that the crew can step calmly ashore from both bow and stern, but not so close that a ripe plum would be squashed between the wall and any of the fenders. Few skippers could guarantee to do this every time, but it is important that you try: not simply in pursuit of excellence as such, but because the closer you get to this ideal, the more leeway you give yourself for the inevitable human misjudgement.

It is not incompetence that causes most skippers to bodge up the approach to their home berths more often than they do a strange one: it is over-confidence—the sort that produces a cavalier approach leaving no room for error. This dashing chap (and many of us see him at times in the bathroom mirror) is so sure of his ability to place his boat neatly alongside that he casually neglects the following basic precautions:

1 Have a heaving line ready coiled for instant use.
2 Have all mooring warps prepared and led as in fig. 61.
3 Have at least one roving fender handy for rapid use.
4 Have the anchor cleared away and ready for letting go.
5 Before leaving a berth, check the operation of the engine in all gears and that the steering works.
6 Give each crew member a specific task to perform.

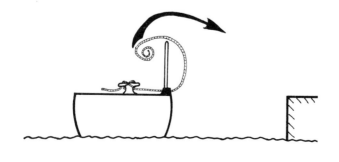

61 Prepare mooring lines by making fast the inboard end led under the lifelines, so that when thrown or taken ashore they lead straight under the lifelines and onto their cleats

Ensure that he is carefully briefed on what is expected of him; and the whole crew appraised of the general plan, so that they know what should be happening at all stages of the operation and can thus forestall any problems that begin to develop.

7 Carefully survey the berth and approaches before heading for it. Make a dummy run past if uncertain of anything, and check wind, stream and obstructions such as moored boats, floating ropes, ledges on a wall, shallow patches etc. Check positions of bollards, ladders and any obstructions to fenders (piles, rough wall)

These simple preparations will take care of most problems likely to arise, and leave your mind free to concentrate totally on achieving the perfect alongside position.

Mooring Up

The ropes to be used for mooring a boat to a quay are shown in fig. 63. It is most important to understand the precise purpose of each one if they are to be secured in the correct place and at the correct angle: these warps do not simply 'tie the boat to the quay to stop her drifting away'.

Head and stern ropes hold the ends of the boat from drifting out; they do not prevent the boat from moving fore and aft along the quay, as is all too often supposed. To allow for movement of the boat in a swell or passing wash, or rise and fall of tide, they should lead at about 45° to the shore and be given the necessary amount of slack to cope with up-and-down movement at each end. If you are berthed outside another boat, extra head and stern ropes should also be taken to the shore so that the weight of your boat is not held on the other's warps. They should lead from right for'ard and aft; if necessary, from the offshore side of bow and stern in order to maintain the correct angle with the quay.

63 The various mooring lines

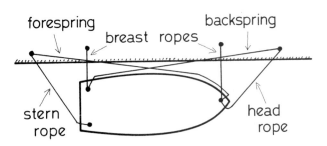

forespring breast ropes backspring

stern rope head rope

Fore and back springs are to prevent the boat from moving fore and aft along the quay. They should lead from right for'ard and aft so as to lie as nearly in line with the quay as feasible, and they should be hauled taut. Movement of the boat in swell or tide is allowed for by making the springs as long as possible.

You will sometimes see springs rigged from amidships, as in fig. 64, but they give far less allowance for rise and fall of tide, and cannot be used for manoeuvring out of a berth, as will be explained in Chapter 6. In a strong tideway they will not hold the boat as squarely in the berth as the springs in fig. 63 as they control the midship section rather than bow and stern.

In a strong head stream the boat will lie back on her head rope and backspring, the former holding the bow in and the latter holding the stern in and the whole boat forward. Without the backspring the boat will lie back on her head rope and the stream will push the bow in, as you can see in fig. 65. These warps can then be adjusted as necessary to keep her exactly where required. If the stream is so strong as to make her rub furiously on her fenders, slackening the head rope slightly will cause the stream to press on the inside of the bow, then run down between boat and quay and push her slightly clear of the wall. Stern rope and forespring must be slack for this to work.

64 **Short springs from amidships: the pontoon floats with the tide, so there is no need to have long lines to allow for rise and fall**

65 **All the pull is on the
head rope, until spring
lines are put on**

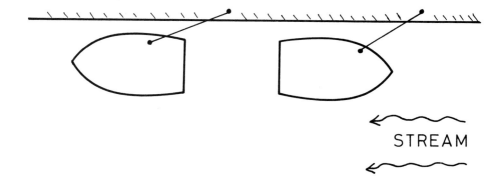

STREAM

For'ard and after breast ropes are rarely left in position as their short lengths and perpendicular leads make them incapable of coping with any movement of the boat. They are, however, useful for mooring temporarily as they hold the boat tightly into the quay. A very slack breast rope rigged to the ladder of a high quay can be useful for hauling in a boat that drifts away from the quay, due to a large tidal range necessitating considerable slack in the main warps.

Temporary berthing in a strong wind or stream along the quay can be made very simply using just one slack breast rope, secured a third of the way from the bow for a head stream and the same distance from the stern for a stream from astern. The boat will lie back on the breast as in fig. 66 and it will hold her securely alongside, due to the angle of its pull.

Getting Alongside

If there is no stream or wind, the basic approach to a berth should be made at about 30° to the line of the quay and with just sufficient speed to maintain good steerage way. The boat should be aimed at the far end of the berth, as that is where you want the bow to end up. On arrival she must then be both stopped and swung parallel to the berth, whereupon the mooring warps can be made fast.

If, on going astern to stop, propeller effects pull the stern in towards the berth, this is precisely how you should come alongside, using your judgement gained from Chapters 1 and 2 to assess when to go astern, and how much power to give her. You will probably need to reinforce the prop effects by swinging the stern in with the rudder just before going astern, while slowing down in neutral (fig. 67).

If propeller effects can be controlled, as with a swivelling prop or twin screws, then this should be the standard approach in the absence of wind or stream. The swivelling prop can be turned on going astern to pull the stern in, and

66 **A breast rope holding the boat alongside**

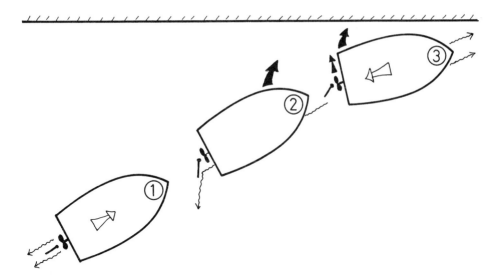

67 **Swinging the stern in**

only the outer of twin screws put astern, to achieve the same. A twin-screw boat should, however, approach the berth going ahead on just the inside prop: partly to keep the speed down, and partly in case the stern needs to be given a swing in before going astern, in order to help the prop effect of the outside screw to get it right in. This will be much easier to do given the assistance of the inside screw's prop effect in ahead gear (fig. 68). Having no rudder, the swivelling prop will need to approach slowly, then give a burst of slipstream if required to start the boat swinging before going astern.

68 **Twin-screw approach**

If, on going astern to stop, propeller effects will pull the stern away from the berth, this approach needs to be

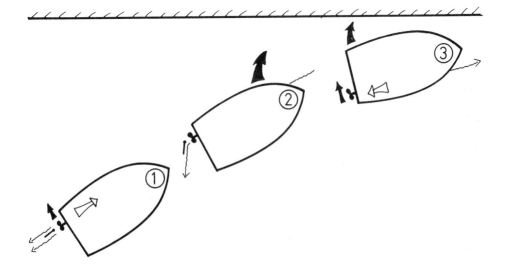

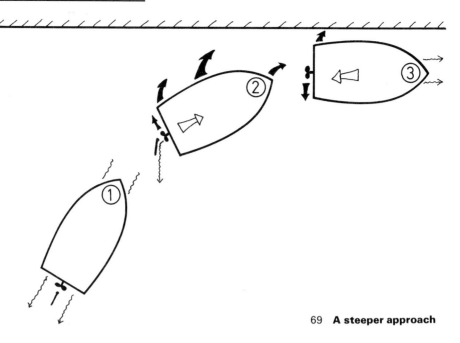

69 A steeper approach

slightly modified. You should make a rather steeper approach and aim for the near end of the berth, thus giving yourself room to give her a fairly hard kick ahead with rudder full over just before arrival. The slipstream will start her stern swinging quickly in towards the berth, and this swing, if judged correctly, will just overcome the outward pull of the prop effects on going astern, sufficiently to bring

70 **This skipper has aimed too far along the berth. Requiring to kick ahead into it, he should have headed further back to give himself room to swing ahead and alongside. You can see the result in fig. 71**

the boat parallel to the quay by the time she has stopped. Your approach speed should be slow enough that the slight forward thrust from this kick ahead just moves her along into the berth and no more (fig. 69). This manoeuvre is slower, but much easier to judge, if you actually bring the boat to a stop in position 2, then kick ahead into the berth; a good policy with a strange boat whose momentum is not known.

If prop effects in ahead are a nuisance, as they may be with an offset or variable pitch propeller, powerful slip-stream must be used to overcome them. Never be afraid to give a good blast ahead with an angled rudder if the boat's attitude needs correcting, whether she is going ahead, astern or is stopped. Many skippers are nervous of doing this, despite the fact that little forward way will be gained if the burst ahead is short enough. The angle of the boat is of paramount importance when coming alongside, and this is nearly always the way to keep it correct. However, see figs 70 and 71.

71 He has also kicked ahead too soon and swung too sharply, ending up beyond the berth and too far off. From the water you can see he is still moving ahead, and the crewman grimly hanging onto the head rope is in grave danger of being yanked into the water

Berthing in a Stream

Whatever direction the stream is flowing, you must remember that it is your movement over the ground during the approach that will take you into the berth—or not, if you get it wrong! Transits must be used, and course allowance made as necessary, to ensure that the boat's movement over the ground does take her towards the berth.

72 **With a strong head stream this catamaran should be aiming much further along the jetty. He could then allow the stream to edge him in as shown in fig. 60, Chapter 3. He did get alongside, with a quick swing and a punch ahead, but this approach leaves no room for error: a breeze onto the jetty, or a slight swing of the stream round the corner of it, would have clobbered him hard onto the knuckle with no room or time to manoeuvre. He is, in effect, viewing the stream as a hindrance to his berthing, whereas the helmsman in fig. 60 is enlisting its help to give him total control over the movement and angle of his boat**

Having said that, you should approach heading into the stream if possible, for the various reasons outlined in Chapter 3. Your approach will then generally be made at a slightly shallower angle than the basic one, aiming somewhat ahead of the berth. The shallow angle, if space permits it, will reduce the sideways set of the stream, making the judgement of its effect rather easier, and slowing down the rate at which things happen. This will, however, reduce the distance the stern must swing in to the berth, and the speed or the angle may have to be adjusted to ensure that prop effects on going astern will not swing the stern in too hard (fig. 72).

With a fairly strong stream it should be possible to come in sideways in a very slow and controlled manner, using throttle to stem the stream and the flow of it over the rudder to make continuous small corrections to attitude as required. You may not even have to go astern at all, simply slowing down and allowing the stream to stop you. The stern can be swung in by using the flow of the stream over the rudder, or perhaps a little slipstream if this is not enough.

In a very strong stream you should continue motoring ahead when alongside, so that the boat remains stationary in relation to the shore while the mooring warps are made fast. All warps, including springs, should be set up properly before stopping the engine, or the stream will sheer the boat and make it very difficult to secure her in the correct position. If you are short-handed, make fast the head rope and backspring first, as they will hold the boat in the correct place and attitude, preventing the bow from swinging out and away in the stream if you get things a bit wrong.

If there is likely to be delay in getting these main warps secured (high wall and no sign of cleats or bollards, perhaps), then try to get a short breast rope to a ladder or ring in the wall, secured as shown in fig. 66. This will hold her snugly in position while you get the main warps sorted out.

Berthing downstream

This is a difficult operation requiring some skill and experience (Chapter 3 explained why). You should avoid berthing in this way unless circumstances force it upon you.

The problem is not so much slowing down, but maintaining the correct attitude (angle to the quay) of the boat while doing so. The importance of attitude when berthing downstream cannot be over-emphasised, as you will not be able to juggle her in on arrival as you can when stemming the stream. If the jetty is long and clear as you are scooting past it sideways, a good blast of slipstream may get you round and alongside, but only with a swivelling prop or twin screws will you be able to hold her in that attitude while going full astern to stop.

In principle a downstream approach should be made at as shallow an angle to the quay as possible, and begun as far upstream from the berth as you can. Throughout the whole approach you must then concentrate on holding her in this attitude, so that you arrive at the berth more or less parallel, close enough to get warps ashore, and travelling as slowly as possible.

During the approach all manoeuvring effects you have available should be used to maintain her attitude and position so that the stream, in effect, carries you directly into the berth. You will have to keep intermittently running her astern to keep down as much as possible your speed over the ground. Each time this throws out her attitude even the slightest bit it must then be immediately corrected, with slipstream if necessary.

On arrival you should immediately make fast a quarter rope, as in fig. 73. This is, in effect, the short temporary breast described earlier, and it will hold the boat into the berth and parallel however strong the stream. It can also be used to slow down and stop her, if surged steadily round a cleat or bollard. The boat should be well fendered right to the bow and stern, as it is very probable that one end or other will sheer into the wall on arrival, however well you have judged the approach.

A single-handed skipper in a small boat would do well to develop skill at berthing downstream, as the close prox-imity of a quarter rope to the helmsman makes it much easier and quicker to get secured than a for'ard breast. If a strong head stream gets on the inside of the bow, it can carry it a long way out from the wall by the time one has clambered out of a cockpit and got for'ard.

Berthing in a cross-stream

In most situations this will only be experienced during the approach, and the use of transits to maintain the correct approach course over the ground will cope with it. On arriving at the berth, it will usually be found that the stream is slack or has been diverted by the jetty to run along it, and a normal berthing manoeuvre can be made as described above. If there is any doubt as to which way the stream will be running in the berth, you should carefully check by observing nearby moorings, or making a dummy run past to see which way the water is flowing.

If you have to berth on an open piled jetty that projects

73 Approaching with the stream

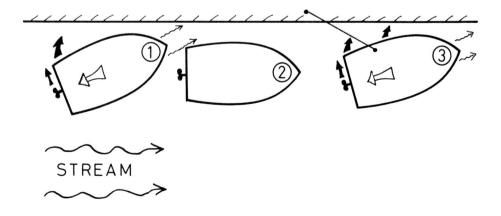

STREAM

into a tideway, however, the cross-stream may be experienced all the way into the berth and great care needs to be taken if the stream is setting you onto it. If it is fairly weak, you should aim to be just clear of the jetty so that the set carries you onto it while you are going astern to stop. This clearance should be no more than necessary or the boat will have time to build up sideways momentum sufficient to come down on the fenders rather hard.

If the stream is of any strength it will not be possible to prevent her coming in sideways at a rate likely to cause damage on arrival, however well fendered. Berthing in such circumstances is not advisable. Even if you manage to get alongside without damage, you will have great difficulty getting away again, and your stay alongside will be uncomfortable at best. If such berthing is necessary you should anchor upstream and drop down into the berth by veering cable. A little tension on the cable will ease the strain on fenders while you are in the berth, and you can haul yourself off with it when leaving.

If the stream is running away from the jetty, it will be difficult to get your stern in against its outward set. You should berth as for extreme prop effects hindering the swing in, and have the stern rope led for'ard outside the rails so that it can be taken ashore from the bow and used to haul the stern in if required. The final swing to parallel the berth should not be made until the bow is virtually touching the jetty or she will be carried away before you can get warps ashore; and it must be made with strong slipstream in ahead gear so that the boat is making up into the stream while she is swinging. If you get it wrong you should be able to work her in on a warp or two, using one of the techniques described in Chapter 6.

Berthing in Wind

As explained in Chapter 3, there are two major differences between the effect of stream and that of wind. The first is that wind affects the attitude of a boat, where stream does not; and the second is that drift from a moderate wind is considerably less than that from a moderate stream. In the absence of stream the approach should generally be made into the wind, although this is not quite so critical as it is when dealing with a stream. If both wind and stream are present, the approach should almost always be made into the stream, with corrections and allowances being made as required for the subsidiary effect of the wind. Only in a howling gale and weak stream should this be reversed, as berthing downwind is much easier to control than berthing downstream.

The drift effect of the wind is most simply allowed for by considering it as a very weak stream, and manoeuvring as described for streams. If both wind and stream prevail, the overall drift can be assessed by combining their influences. The effect of wind on the attitude of a boat when berthing, however, is less simple.

Wind from ahead

As the boat will be approaching at an angle to the quay, this wind will in fact blow on the outside of the bow and swing it in towards the berth. A great many skippers panic on seeing their bows swinging rapidly into the wall, and go astern in the fond hopes of reducing the impact. This is quite the worst thing you can do. Propeller effects may try to pull the stern in, but the draw of the wind—even from this angle—will pull it out more strongly, dragging the bow in even more rapidly. The further the bow swings from the wind, the faster will it blow in, and the nervous skipper who goes astern while still some way from the berth could end up arriving at right angles to his intended position, blowing merrily sideways along the quay completely out of control. You do not need to be psychic to foresee the result of this if other boats are moored downwind of the berth.

The cure for this is a good blast of slipstream to drive her head out again. If you watch the bow carefully, you will detect this swing in time to straighten her up with little effect on your approach. The further the bow blows off before you correct, the closer to the berth she will end up after the correction, as you will be swinging the stern inwards to more or less where the bow reached. This effect can be useful if you realise that you are too far out: successively allowing the bow to swing in, then driving it out again, causing the boat to move sideways towards the wall (fig. 74).

Wind from astern

This will tend to blow the stern away from the quay during the approach as well as drive the boat forward. With a head stream to slow her down, slipstream can safely be used to kick her round and alongside, and the draw of the wind utilised to hold her straight while going astern to stop.

If there is no head stream the angle of approach should be shallower than normal, so as to keep the wind as near directly astern as you can. You must keep the speed down during the approach with intermittent bursts astern, and if the effect of draw pulls her bodily away from the berth, this must be corrected with slipstream to kick her ahead and

74 The head of the 'dotted' boat begins to blow off when she coasts into position (2). Boat A panics and goes astern, while B keeps his head and gives a good blast of slipstream over his angled rudder. You can see clearly the results. The only hope now for A's skipper is to go full astern and hope the wind will draw him round and clear of the moored boats so that he can go right away and try the approach again.

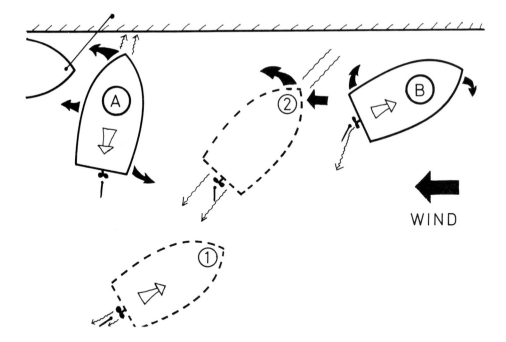

inwards. With the boat kicked round alongside the wall, the draw of the wind can then be utilised to hold her there while going astern to stop (fig. 75). Because of the wind's draw on the stern, it is much easier to berth downwind than downstream. You are also more likely to encounter a berth, such as the fuelling berth on the right of fig. 76, which you will have to enter downwind.

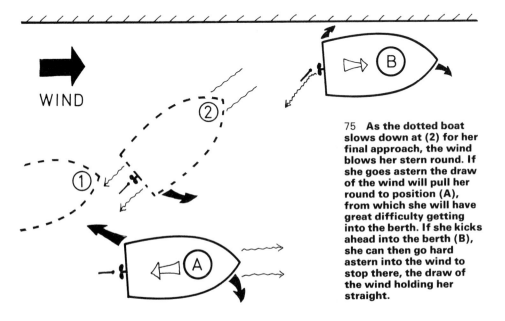

75 **As the dotted boat slows down at (2) for her final approach, the wind blows her stern round. If she goes astern the draw of the wind will pull her round to position (A), from which she will have great difficulty getting into the berth. If she kicks ahead into the berth (B), she can then go hard astern into the wind to stop there, the draw of the wind holding her straight.**

Wind onto quay

This will blow the bow in, and also push the boat bodily sideways towards the berth. Approach should be made as for a stream running onto the jetty, and corrections to attitude made as for a head wind.

If strong onshore winds are expected to blow up during your stay alongside, it is good policy to let go an anchor during the approach, so that it can be used to both ease the strain on fenders and haul her off when leaving. A steep approach should be made so as to get the anchor almost straight out from the berth and the cable veered rapidly so that it does not affect handling while berthing. It can, however, be snubbed to hold the bow if required, while the stern is swung in.

Wind off quay

Approach as in a stream off the quay, but bearing in mind that wind will blow the bow off very rapidly as you swing the stern in. Slipstream must be used to keep her head up into the wind during the approach, which should be steeper still than recommended for a stream off the quay, in order to minimise the effect of wind on the bow. Getting the stern in will be less difficult than with a stream, due to the wind blowing the bow round rather than carrying the whole

76 **This fuel berth, right, can only be approached from one direction**

boat away. If you get it a bit wrong, study Chapter 6 (beforehand!) and consider how you can use the draw of the wind while in astern gear.

In all situations where there is a likelihood of the wind blowing any part of the boat away from the wall, it is most important that warps be made fast ashore as soon as possible. Hence the preparations detailed at the beginning of the chapter.

Berthing Stern First

You may find an awkward berth that cannot be entered by going ahead. Making a sternboard into an alongside berth is not difficult with twin screws or a swivelling prop as the angle of the boat can be controlled throughout the operation. You must think carefully about the effect of wind during a sternboard, and also the behaviour of the boat on going *ahead* to stop. With a single prop it is most important that you keep sufficient way on for the rudder to steer right until the last minute. You should be able to stop her very quickly with a hard burst ahead, but the rudder must be positioned as required before the slipstream hits it, not left in the position for steering backwards.

The Use of Bow Thrust

An easier way of positioning the bow exactly where you want it, and particularly of holding it up against a wind, would be hard to imagine. This would be especially useful in conjunction with prop effects, for moving the boat bodily against a wind or stream that is setting her off the berth, or onto it.

Leaving a Berth

The basic problem here is the fact that a boat swings her stern away from a turn when going ahead, and her bow away when going astern, so you must make some space between boat and wall before you can turn away from it and proceed. If wind or stream is tending to push her off the wall, you can simply let go all the mooring warps and allow her to drift clear of the berth. In all other circumstances you will need to do something rather more positive to get clear, and techniques for doing so will be found in Chapter 6, along with various methods for getting into awkward berths and rescuing mistakes.

5 Anchoring and Mooring

Anchoring

The secret of secure anchoring lies in understanding precisely how an anchor and cable work, and thus how they should be set out on the sea bed. In fig. 77 we have the classic picture of how anchor and cable should lie on the bottom: the anchor firmly dug in and the cable ranged out in a straight line, partly to ensure a horizontal pull on the anchor and partly to add its own weight and drag in the seabed to the holding power.

The moment the boat swings round with a changing tidal stream or wind, however, this neat arrangement will be upset. In fig. 78 you can see that as the boat swings the cable is drawn round in an arc, the extent of which depends on the strength of wind or stream. The boat then lies largely to the weight and drag of the arc of cable rather than the anchor directly.

This formation has less holding power than when anchor and cable are in line, so you should always endeavour to

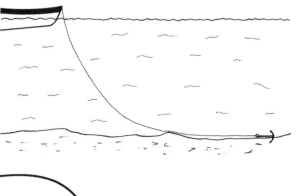

77 Lying to a single anchor

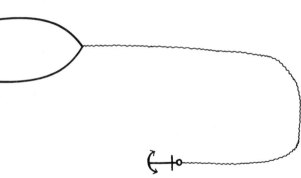

78 After the boat has swung round

have them in line when lying to the stronger stream. In a river or estuary this will usually be the ebb, reinforced by river water so as to run harder than the flood; or it may be the stream that is running with a strong wind. To achieve this, there are two quite different ways of bringing up to a single anchor, depending on whether you are stemming the stronger or weaker stream on approaching an anchorage.

Bringing up to a single anchor

The approach to an anchorage should always be made into the stream or wind, for the same reasons as explained for berthing alongside. If this happens to be the strongest you will lie to, the boat should be stopped just beyond the chosen spot and put astern. The moment she begins to move astern the anchor should be let go and the cable veered steadily as she continues to back down. As the way comes on her the prop should be put into neutral and the stream or wind allowed to take her back, so that she does not move too rapidly. When the required amount of cable is out, it should be snubbed and the boat allowed to settle. You should then give her a short burst of astern power to straighten the cable and ensure that the anchor is well dug in.

If two main anchors are carried in hawse pipes, you must be sure to let go the one that will lead out to windward as she drifts. If the leeward one is let go its cable will drag under the hull as she swings, then drifts beam-on to the wind. If the wind is dead ahead on the approach to the anchorage, give her a slight sheer before letting go, so as to ensure that the anchor let go is to weather. The same applies if a single anchor is let go on one side of the stem, particularly if bowsprits and bobstays protrude (fig. 79).

79 **Straight stems and bobstays can catch on the anchor cable**

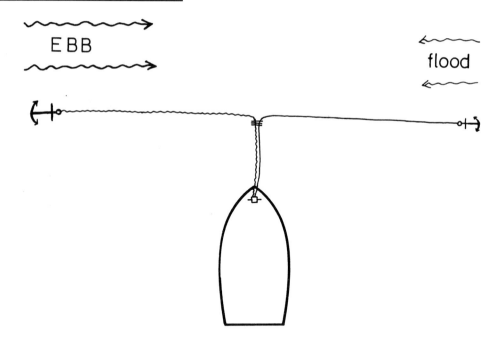

EBB

flood

If the approach is made into the weaker stream, continue to motor slowly ahead through the chosen spot and let go the anchor as she passes it. Then continue ahead slowly under engine, veering the cable as she goes, making sure that it runs out quickly enough to remain clear of the hull. The boat should be stopped in time to prevent the cable coming taut under the hull when the required amount is out, and it should then be made fast.

Mooring to Two Anchors

The amount of swinging room required by a boat lying to a single anchor can be considerable in strong streams and winds. In many anchorages these days, especially where there are permanent moorings, this sort of space is just not available. In such situations you may have to *moor ship* with two anchors, one laid upstream and the other downstream of the berth. Done properly this should give the boat much the same reduced swinging area as a permanent mooring.

The layout of anchors and cables can be seen in fig. 80. If one of the two anchors is a lighter kedge, you should lay the main anchor and cable to hold the boat against the stronger stream. There are two ways of mooring ship, and you should choose the one that enables you most easily to do this.

80 **On two anchors, the heavier one holding her against the stronger strain**

Dropping moor

As its name implies, this technique involves letting go the main anchor and dropping back from it with the wind or stream, just as described for letting go a single anchor when the prevailing stream is the stronger. This time, however, the sternboard is continued past the berth until twice the calculated amount of cable has been veered: the cable is then snubbed and the anchor set. The second anchor is let go underfoot and the boat motored or hauled back to the chosen berth, hauling in the first warp and veering the second as she goes. Once back at the chosen berth, there should be equal scope for each anchor. The two warps should then be lashed together with a racking seizing and both veered until the join is well below the keel. The boat can then swing round the junction of the two warps in a very small arc, without fouling either of them. She will lie to the main anchor and cable against the stronger stream, and to the kedge on the weaker one.

Running moor

Again, the name describes the technique. Let go the main anchor on the run, as described for a single anchor when the prevailing stream is the weaker, but continue motoring slowly ahead until twice the calculated amount of cable has been veered. Then let go the kedge underfoot and drop back until the two warps are middled. Secure as for the dropping moor.

If a crosswind is experienced it must be corrected for in steering, so as to ensure that the warps lie fairly up and down stream. The dinghy in fig. 81 is actually secured by her painter to a ground chain, but it shows more or less how cables would lie if she was moored to her own two anchors. The riser would need to be longer to keep the cables well below the keel and allow her to swing round without fouling them.

81 The boat on the right, especially, needs a longer line down to the ground chain

Weighing Anchor

Simply reverse all these procedures, using engines as necessary to ease the strain on the cables, particularly if they are being recovered by hand. Be careful not to overrun a cable or you might wrap it round the prop, especially if it is nylon.

Mooring to a Buoy

This is rather easier than anchoring, except that the bow must be stopped close enough to the buoy for it to be picked up. The approach should be made into wind or stream, and the bow stopped to one side of the buoy so that propeller effects will swing it to the buoy while going astern to stop.

In very strong headwinds it can be almost impossible to hold a high bow close to the buoy long enough to make fast, and it can often be better to approach the mooring stern first into the wind, so that the draw of the wind on her stern will hold her in position. Go slowly astern close past the buoy and hold her stopped with the bow next to it while she is made fast. You should come up on the side of the buoy from which she will drift clear (with wind and/or stream) when you let her swing round; and ensure, while the mooring is being made fast, that she remains in such a position by using prop and rudder. You may have to sheer her in the desired direction with a brief kick of slipstream before allowing her to swing. Make fast first with a slip-rope (both ends on board), to hold her while you secure properly. It can be retained and used for slipping from the mooring when you leave.

Mooring Bow and Stern

In very restricted spaces it may be necessary to moor the boat by her head and stern, so that she cannot swing at all. There are two basic types of such moorings, and both can require considerable handling skill to get into when conditions are difficult.

Buoys and piles

Berthing between buoys or piles can be approached similarly to anchoring, in that you can either make fast to the upstream one then drop back and secure to the other, or you can first put a line on the downstream one and then motor up to the other and make fast. The choice depends on conditions making one easier than the other: fore-and-aft moorings being equally strong, we do not have to consider which direction of stream is the faster.

In general, if wind or stream is directly in line with the pair of moorings, the dropping method is better, as you can simply approach and secure to the upstream mooring (or pile) as though it were a single mooring, then veer warp until the stern is close enough to the downstream one to make fast. The boat is securely held in roughly the right place all the time, and any small adjustments that need making to the position of the stern can be done very simply with prop and rudder. If the bow swings off a lot as the head rope is veered it should be snubbd as required to allow the boat to settle into line. Be certain to keep the stern rope clear of the prop.

If wind and/or stream are to one side, however, things are rather more difficult, particularly if the berth is hemmed in by other boats. In general, the running type of moor will be preferable in such circumstances, with the approach made at an angle from leeward so as to make fast the stern to the downstream mooring first, before proceeding to manoeuvre the bow onto the upstream one (fig. 82). This will be much easier if the stern line is passed forward outside the rails and rigging so that it can be made fast as the bow slowly passes the first mooring. The crew must then hold it up well clear of the prop as the boat manoeuvres to the upstream one. The line must be slack, however, so that it will not pull on the boat and restrict manoeuvring, as the stern may need to be kicked hard over to get the bow up into the wind at the upstream mooring.

There is a danger of getting into terribly expensive trouble should you fail to get the bow secured to the upstream

82 **Between piles, in a cross-wind**

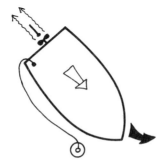

mooring. The boat could then, in a strong wind or stream, swing back round on her stern line, cutting through any nearby moored boats like a scythe. This risk can be reduced by having the stern line ready for instant casting off, so you can then motor hard up into the wind and get clear for another try if space permits.

You could also let go the anchor on a short length of cable (just sufficient to hold the bow), and keep her out of trouble while you send the bow line across by dinghy. A heavy anchor and cable is useful for this trick as very little scope is needed to hold her. The anchor should be buoyed in case it picks up a mooring chain. Being aware of the dangers in this sort of manoeuvre, you should have the foredeck hand alerted to the possibility of instantly letting go the anchor, as the smallest delay could be disastrous.

The dinghy should also be ready for instant use, but keep it on a very short painter (or alongside) or you could find the boat going one side of a pile and the dinghy the other! It happens. This type of preparation is also wise if approaching a single buoy in strong winds or streams when hemmed in by other moored boats.

If there is room to leeward of the piles it would be better to approach more steeply so that sideways drift across to the head pile can be controlled more precisely by balancing slipstream against wind or stream.

With a head stream and following wind, it should be relatively easy to haul her astern to the after pile using the draw of the wind on her stern.

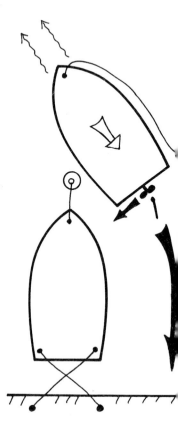

83   **Fore-and-aft moorings on both sides of a river channel, like these, are quite common. You can see how little space there is on the bank side for manoeuvring. If your permanent berth is like this, life is much easier if you can leave a dinghy between the moorings with the yacht's head and stern ropes already secured to the moorings and the ends lying coiled in the dinghy. You can then simply come alongside it, pick them up and make fast both ends of the boat immediately**

84   **Backing in past a mooring buoy**

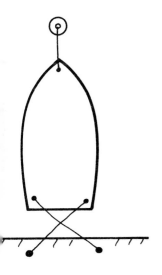

Getting away

In the simplest situation, with wind and stream coming from ahead, you can let go the stern line and slip from the upstream mooring just as you would from a single mooring. With the close proximity of the after pile to the stern, it may be advisable to give her a sheer in the right direction before slipping the headrope, so that you can motor hard clear away before being carried back onto it. With the wind on the beam, and room to swing to leeward, much the same will suffice. If wind and/or stream are from astern, however, life is not so easy and a springing technique will need to be employed in order to manoeuvre into a suitable position from which to leave: see fig. 94 in Chapter 6.

Mediterranean Mooring

This style of berthing is virtually standard in the Medi-terranean, and becoming more popular elsewhere as mooring spaces get increasingly crowded. One end of the boat is made fast to a quay and the other to an off-lying mooring or the anchor.

Traditionally, boats lie stern to the quay, which involves picking up the mooring at the bow, or letting go the anchor, and then making a sternboard into the very narrow gap between neighbouring boats. With no wind or stream this is a fairly straightforward matter of assessing how your boat will move astern, then rounding up clear of the buoy in such a position that you can motor astern close past it, make fast a head rope, then continue into the berth. A boathook should be handy to pick up the buoy.

With a single fixed prop and rudder, you may need to correct your attitude from time to time with a brief kick ahead, when she swings off course. Stern ropes should be crossed as shown, so that they also act as springs, and the head rope should be brought aft outside of rails and rigging so that it can be made fast to the buoy as the stern passes it. This is a wise precautionary measure should the bow drift clear of the buoy; also the lower freeboard aft will make the job easier. The headrope can then be taken in steadily as the boat backs into the berth. In fig. 84 you can see the position a boat with single right-handed prop should take up, and the line along which her sternboard will take her. With a left-handed prop you would make your sternboard from the other side of the buoy.

A wind blowing off the quay will assist this sternboard, drawing the stern of the boat towards itself. If it is blowing along the quay, it should be remembered that the stern will swing towards it while backing and the boat should be positioned accordingly. If the stern swings upwind excessively, the boat can be drifted back into line by stopping the prop and snubbing the head rope. Keeping a little weight on the head rope will straighten her line by preventing the bow blowing off, thus reducing the draw of the wind on the stern.

If the wind is blowing onto the quay you should approach along the line of buoys and stop at yours where it is just to leeward of your bow. The headrope can be made fast and the wind allowed to blow the stern round into the berth. If space is restricted you may need to rig a backspring from the stern to the buoy and work her into the berth (as shown in fig. 111, Chapter 6) in order to get her stern downwind. In fig. 85 you can see the sort of tight space you are likely to find in a marina. In a strong wind the best thing to do here would be to pick up a buoy on the other side, opposite your berth, with a slip-rope; then lower yourself astern into the berth. If there is nothing up wind, it may be wise to let go a buoyed anchor well clear of the moorings and do the same.

If you have to anchor the manoeuvre is slightly different

85 Tight marina berths with buoys to avoid

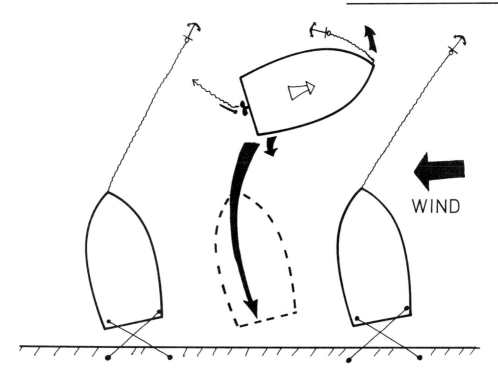

WIND

86 **Dropping and backing in, with cross-wind**

and some care is needed in choosing the place to let go. You should veer the same amount of cable as you would for lying to a single anchor, so if you let go too close to the berth and arrive at the wall with insufficient cable out, you will have to go out and start again!

The other point you need to consider is the positions of your neighbours' anchors, as unbelievable trouble and tangles can ensue if you lay your cable across one of theirs (which, in my experience, is probably already across the next one along). In a cross-wind or stream, all the boats will be lying down wind or stream of their anchors, and you must gauge as accurately as you can where these anchors are so that you let yours go between them. Buoying the anchor is absolutely essential when lying stern-to like this, and you should paint an anchor on the buoy or someone will certainly moor up to it in the middle of the night.

The basic technique is to approach along the line of boats, into the wind or stream, then let go the anchor in the chosen spot, snub it when enough cable is out to grip, and motor her round it until she lies in position for the sternboard into the berth (fig. 86). The suitable position will depend on prop effects and wind, and will generally be as for a sternboard from a buoy. The cable can be snubbed as required to hold her head up to the wind during the sternboard.

If space permits and prop effects are controllable (twin-screw or swivelling prop), you may be able to simply round up off the berth, then let go the anchor and back straight in, particularly in the absence of wind or stream.

If you want to use two anchors they should be let go on either side of where a single one would be, so that their cables will make an angle of about 30° when the boat is in her berth. This will increase noticeably the risk of entanglement with the neighbours' cables, but will hold the boat more firmly and securely in her berth.

The approach should be made more or less as for letting go a single anchor, and the anchor on the side away from the berth let go first so that the boat can swing away from it when the time comes. When you reach position for the second anchor it should be let go, then the first one immediately snubbed and slipstream used to turn on it until the boat is in position for the sternboard. Both cables should be veered as required to keep her straight as she backs in, the weather one clearly controlling the position of the bow in a wind (fig. 87).

Some skippers find it easier to berth bow to the quay as the boat can be more easily controlled on the way in. This is not always the case, especially in strong winds when the

87 **Using two anchors**

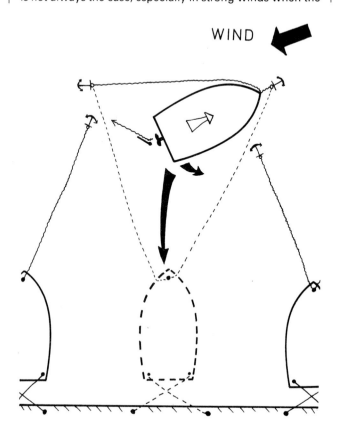

WIND

88 **Mooring between piles: almost all boats went in bows first**

traditional method enables the rapidly drifting bow to be controlled by a head rope or anchor, and the attitude and position of the boat by working the draw of the wind and prop effects against this. It also means using a kedge over the stern if a buoy is not available, and this will not provide the security of a heavy bower anchor and cable. Bows-to is commonly done by small boats and dinghies when berthing on a crowded wall or jetty. The technique consists of lobbing the anchor over the stern at the crucial moment as you head directly towards the wall, allowance being made as necessary for wind or stream.

Some marina berths have piles for the offshore mooring, as you can see in fig. 88. Entering between these involves the same basic technique as for a buoy, but correction must be made for the fact that there will be two piles, one either side of the berth, instead of a single buoy ahead of it. The head rope must go first onto the upwind or upstream one, then the bow drifted or manoeuvred to attach the other before making the sternboard. In any strength of wind or stream this could be rather tricky, and a better method will be found in Chapter 6, fig. 111.

Anchoring in Strong Winds

Although a properly set anchor and cable should hold a boat securely in all normal conditions, it may not be sufficient if you are caught out in an exposed anchorage in a real blow. Even in a reasonably sheltered anchorage, strong winds blowing against a fast stream can cause a boat to yaw badly at anchor, particularly if she has much windage for'ard and little underwater body, or a very short keel. Some auxiliary sailing yachts are particularly bad in this respect, often combining considerable windage of spars and rigging for'ard with short fin-keels; power cruisers may have even more windage. Those that tend to sail about constantly snub their cables, putting great strain on fittings and the holding ability of the anchor.

Yawing at anchor can be considerably reduced by letting go a second anchor on just enough scope that it drags along the bottom, so damping the movement of the bow. If the yawing threatens to drive the boat onto a bank or other danger, this anchor should be put down when the bow is at the end of the yaw away from the danger. It will then prevent her sheering across that way.

If the cable is at very long stay (pulled out taut) as the boat lies hard back on it, the catenary can be improved by sliding a 'traveller' weight down the cable, so putting extra weight into the bight of it. This will soften the shock loads experienced with a taut cable, and also keep the anchor stock and more cable on the seabed. A pig of ballast is about the minimum weight that will have any effect on even a fairly small boat.

If conditions are really severe a *hurricane hawse* or *open moor* may be set in order to use the full holding power of two anchors and cables. The anchors are laid in the same way as for berthing stern-to with both anchors, but the angle between them can profitably be reduced. The closer they are together, the less strain will be on each one. The strain can be reduced further, if necessary, by steaming slowly into wind between the cables (fig. 89).

If you are already lying to a single anchor when the wind is forecast to shift into an exposed quarter and blow up severely, you can motor towards a suitable position for the second anchor (weighing the cable of the first as you go), then let go and veer both cables in readiness for the blow. It should be apparent that this will be much easier if the second anchor is on the side of the bow nearest the expected wind shift, as the first anchor wll not then have to be weighed. With the first left where it is, you can simply let go the second so that the line joining them is at right angles to the expected windshift; then when it comes you can adjust the cables to take up a position as shown by the dotted lines in fig. 90.

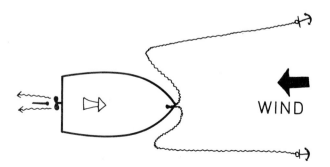

89 **Relieving the strain on the anchors**

WIND

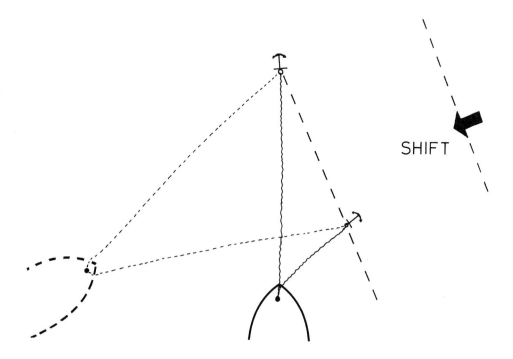

90 Anticipating a wind shift

For this reason it is sound policy with two anchors in hawsepipes to always use the one opposite the expected windshift, so that the other will be free to use in a hurricane hawse if required. In the northern hemisphere the passage of a depression causes the wind to veer from SE through S to NW, so the port anchor should be normally used. In the southern hemisphere the wind shifts the other way (backs) and the starboard anchor should be used. If you lay a metaphorical compass rose over the top of fig. 90 this should be clear.

Another way of using two anchors in severe weather is to shackle them in tandem on the same cable, a technique much favoured by writers who have had to use it in earnest. The merit of this is that each anchor directly helps to prevent the other from either dragging or pulling up out of the seabed. They should have chain between them, and ideally be far enough apart to enable the first to be weighed before the second has to be broken out: something in the region of one and a half times the depth. At least, have enough chain between to get the first anchor on deck while the other is still in the water. It may be found quite impossible to break out two heavy anchors together if they have been well dug in.

Dragging Anchor

Taking proper anchor bearings will show up any dragging of the anchor over a period of time, but there are some quick indications that are useful. If you lean over the bow and hold the cable with your hand outboard of the stem, you should be able to feel the vibration of a dragging anchor. This can be easily confused with the harmless rumbling of cable being dragged out in a bight if you are lying as shown in fig. 78. If you are certain your cable lies as in fig. 77 (immediately after anchoring and sitting back on the cable, for instance), then such rumbling will denote dragging. If you are not certain how the cable lies, you will find that a dragging anchor produces a more intermittent, jarring vibration than a dragging cable, as the anchor tends

91 **Two heavy barges lying to one's anchor; however, there are crew aboard both**

to move in jumps as the cable tightens, rather than steadily sliding along the bottom as the cable will.

In a strong headwind a dragging anchor will show itself by allowing the bow to blow downwind. Instead of lying head-to-wind like everyone else, you will be lying beam-on to it. It is never wise to raft up with other boats on a single anchor, due to the extra strain imposed on its holding. This is a rather popular habit but is no more seamanlike than using too small an anchor and cable. Consider the strain on the single anchor in fig. 91.

The initial response to a dragging anchor should be to veer more cable, but once an anchor starts dragging it is usually reluctant to dig itself back in. As soon as the extra cable has caused the anchor to bite (which may only be temporary), start the engine and go astern on the cable to try and dig the anchor back in properly. If this does not work, you will have to weigh and re-anchor.

Nylon Anchor Warps

The use of nylon for an anchor warp does not, in principle, alter any of the techniques we have discussed. It does, however, have quite different qualities to chain cable, and it is important to understand these.

Nylon cushions snubbing of the anchor by its elasticity rather than by the catenary curve of chain cable. This causes it to always 'grow' or pull out straight when there is a long scope out, in any weight of wind or stream, thus giving the boat a greatly enlarged swinging circle. Its lack of weight also allows more violent yawing, and makes it more likely to involve itself in the propeller if the boat rides over it.

6 Working with Warps and Springs

If we consider the many forces that we can bring to bear for the purpose of moving or turning a boat under power—wind, stream, propeller thrust, slipstream, paddlewheel effect and so on—and imagine the effects of these forces acting around a fixed pivot point like a very powerful lever, it should be apparent that by securing one point of the boat to the shore or seabed we can add a whole new dimension to the business of manoeuvring in tight spaces.

It is most important, however, to understand what is happening when you apply thrust to a boat that is secured to a warp. A variety of complex forces come into play, and you must appreciate roughly where they all are and what they are doing or all attempts to pull off a clever springing operation will come to naught.

The two basic principles that lie behind all springing manoeuvres were explained in Chapter 1. They are:

1 The more difficult a boat is to move, the greater will be slipstream and propeller effects.
2 When turning, a boat pivots around a point one-third of her length back from her leading end.

To keep explanations simple throughout this chapter, let us call the first principle *thrust effect* and the second *turning effect*. Now let us see how we can use these for some very useful manoeuvring.

Springing out of a Berth

This is fairly straightforward, if done properly, and can be used to swing either bow or stern away from a wall, or another boat, preparatory to leaving a berth.

Springing the stern off

The essence of this is to hold the bow firmly with the forespring (a line from the bow aft) so that it cannot move ahead. Force exerted on the shoreward quarter of the boat will then cause the stern to swing round away from the wall (fig. 92). Any sort of force can be used to swing the

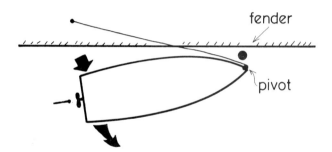

fender

pivot

92 **Springing out the stern**

stern, as long as it can be made to move the inner quarter away from the wall: suitable prop effects, the slipstream, an offshore wind or a tug. Even a following wind or stream will do so if the stern can be moved out slightly to catch it and bring the pressure onto the inner quarter. A push off with a boathook would suffice for a small boat, although a following stream would probably push the stern out anyway as it tried to squeeze in between the stern and the wall

As soon as the stern is far enough out, the spring line can be slipped and pulled aboard and the boat motored clear astern. The distance the stern should be swung out will depend on factors that might restrict the boat's back-wards course into clear water: an onshore wind, the pres-ence of moorings or other boats, prop effects on going astern. Anything opposing the swing, such as adverse prop effects, onshore wind or headstream, will anyway limit the angle you can spring her to. If so, you may need some careful fendering for'ard to prevent the bow scraping as you move astern, although this can be minimised by going astern hard and fast. Before beginning the springing oper-ation you should assess how far out you are likely to get, and how she will behave when you go astern on getting there. Bear in mind that if the stern pulls out due to wind or prop effects, the bow will swing in.

The pivot point must be right for'ard so that the whole length of the boat can swing round it. If it is brought aft, turning effect will cause the bow to move in as the stern goes out. If the bow is prevented from moving in by the wall, it will not be possible to swing the stern out, however much thrust is applied to it (fig. 93).

This technique can be used very effectively to spring your stern out from between two piles when a following or beam wind prevents you from simply slipping and motoring off: see Chapter 5. The head rope holds the bow, rather than wall and fender, while you go ahead on a backspring rigged from the leeward side back to the after pile. If the wind is from aft, the stern line can be eased slowly to control the swing of the stern (fig. 94).

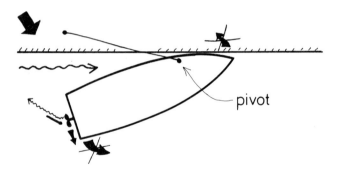

93 **Spring line too far aft**

Springing the bow off

The principle is exactly the same, but thrust on the inner bow is worked against a backspring from the stern. All the comments made above apply.

If, however, this thrust cannot be exerted directly on the bow, it must be exerted indirectly by means of prop effects hauling the outside of the stern aft and inwards. The outer of twin screws, or an outward-turning prop offset on the outer quarter would do the job nicely while going astern. A swivelling prop or one with suitable paddlewheel effect would make a reasonable job, while any other config-uration would provide little or no such pull on the stern. The closeness of the force to the pivoting point would, whatever the configuration, reduce the turning con-siderably compared with that achieved by the same force springing off the stern. With opposing influences such as onshore wind or following stream, it may not be possible to get the bow off at all.

By and large, unless the stern projects beyond the end of the wall so that the pivot point can be moved forward away from the thrust as in fig. 95, thus enabling the stern to swing inwards round the pivot, springing the bow off with prop effects alone is a lot less effective than springing the stern off. It does, however, give the benefit of being able to motor off ahead instead of astern, although care must be taken to avoid clobbering exposed props against the wall.

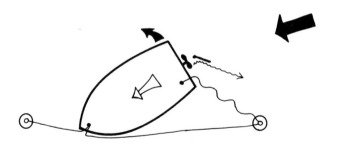

94 **Springing out from between piles**

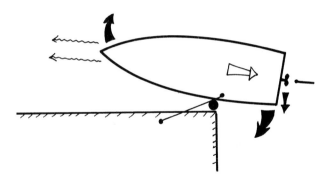

95 Pivoting round a corner

Springing into a Berth

You do not often see this very useful trick, although it is an excellent way of rescuing a misjudged berthing operation that ends up too far off the jetty. It is also often the only seamanlike way of getting into a berth that is too tight for a textbook approach.

Springing the stern in

A common situation is where a skipper has failed to get his stern into the berth, usually through misjudging the swing required to overcome an adverse propeller effect, or often by over-confidently swinging sharp round into a berth without bothering to settle down on a proper approach course.

The common response to this situation—especially if a breeze of wind is blowing the boat out of the berth—is a flurry of tangled stern lines being frantically hurled into the water. If the wind is also pushing her ahead, the situation invariably disintegrates rapidly as the skipper keeps going astern to stay clear of the boat ahead of him. This originally minor misjudgement can easily turn rapidly into a real disaster, unless the skipper slips the head rope and goes hard astern right out of it and tries again.

A far more controlled solution is to quickly pass a forespring ashore, leading aft from a point about one-third of the way back from the bow, and go slow ahead on this with the helm over to swing the stern in (fig. 96). Slipstream will cause the stern to swing in and turning effect will bring the bow out, both pivoting around the lead of the spring. The angle of the spring will prevent forward movement so that the thrust of the prop is forced to push the boat sideways into the wall. The angle of the boat as she comes into the berth can be controlled quite precisely by swinging the stern in or out, after which propulsion and steering can be used to hold her alongside against the spring while she is properly moored up.

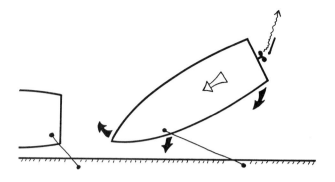

96 Springing the stern in

There is much to be said for having such a spring always prepared when coming alongside, partly in case of the above problem and partly because it is a good way of holding a boat in position in adverse conditions while proper mooring warps are made fast. I call it a *turning forespring*.

The significance of the pivot position is that it maximises turning effect, so enabling you to easily correct the attitude of the boat. If the pivot is right for'ard, turning effect will be zero as the bow cannot swing out; the boat will maintain her attitude and the thrust of the prop will drive her bow into the wall. If the pivot point is further aft, turning efficiency will be reduced and the boat will move forward more during the evolution, which could pose problems if another boat is moored close ahead. In figs 97, 98 and 99 you can see this turning forespring used to get a large motorsailer into a tight marina berth.

97 This large ketch approached her berth from the right of the picture and had to enter at this angle due to lack of space for turning in the channel. She has put her bow close to the end of the pontoon and sent a hand ashore with a turning forespring rigged from amidships. This was secured at the end of the pontoon and the boat continued her turn into the berth

98   As she swung round into the berth, her stern inevitably swung away from the pontoon towards the neighbouring boat as she went astern to stop with her right-handed prop. The turning forespring has caught under the corner of the pontoon and stopped her too soon. However, it still works, and she is here going ahead with rudder over to port to work herself alongside using the pull of the spring

99   And here she is neatly alongside with no shouting, pushing or pulling. The spring has been cleared from the corner and now holds her precisely in the right place while the other warps are secured. As this is his permanent berth, the skipper has been able to secure the spring beforehand at exactly the right length to enable him to spring her in without having to leave the helm. His one crew has remained ashore to secure mooring warps when he is alongside. A tidy and seamanlike job

Springing the bow in

If the bow needs to be brought in, the manoeuvre will work in much the same way, by going astern on a back-spring led from a point the same distance for'ard of the stern, but only if prop effects will induce the stern to swing out. Even then the attitude of the boat will not be con-trollable (except with twin screws or a swivelling prop) in the way it is when going ahead on a spring, when slip-stream can be used to swing the stern either way. The turning effect gained by a boat going ahead on such a spring is flexible enough to be used for swinging the bow in as well as out, and this would be the better method for correcting either misjudgement. Go astern first if necessary to give room for the bow to swing past another boat or corner of a jetty. It would be a mistake to try bringing the bow in using a conventional forespring led to the stem, as then all control of the stern would be lost, due to the lack of turning effect.

Springing Round a Corner

To get round a very tight corner we can also employ springs in a similar manner to the techniques already described. The boat does not, however, pivot simply around the lead of the spring, but swings (with the warp) in an arc round the point on shore to which the spring is made fast.

Turning ahead

In fig. 100 you can see how a large boat can be sprung out of a narrow harbour entrance when there is insufficient room for her to turn normally in the channel outside. The spring can be rigged as you pass through the entrance, and

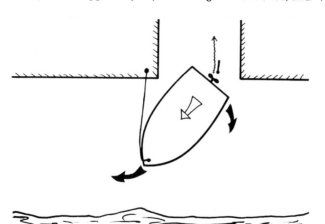

100 Turning tight, going ahead

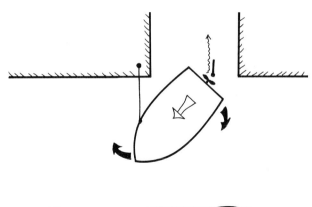

101 Turning with spring rigged aft of bow

must be paid out and kept slack until you are certain that the stern will swing clear of the wall. You can then take a couple of turns on the spring line to hold her, put the helm hard over and give her some slipstream.

If the channel outside is little wider than the length of the boat, the turn can be tightened even more by bringing the lead of the spring aft by one-third the length of the boat, as described above for a turning spring. This will bring the pivot point back nearer the middle of the channel, and also enable the bow to swing round inside the pivot, causing her to finish up closer to the entrance on completing the turn (fig. 101). The turning effect that this gives will enable you to control the attitude of the boat as she goes round, and this would be a good way to come out and get alongside the outer wall all in one operation.

Turning astern

This is a particularly useful manoeuvre for getting out of a cramped marina berth, such as in fig. 102. In fig. 103 you

102 A short backspring, rigged to the pontoon in preparation for turning out of the berth

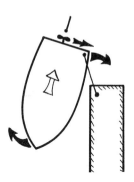

can see a short backspring rigged to the corner of the jetty or pontoon, and the boat is run slow astern against this. Although the same limitations of prop effects apply as were discussed in the section on springing the bow off, more effect will be gained in this situation due to the freedom of the stern to continue swinging into open water. Improving the torque by moving the pivot point forward (see fig. 95) will, however, cause her to swing more readily. You can see the manoeuvre in figs 104, 105 and 106.

103 **Turning round a pontoon**

104 **A short spring line from the stern quarter nearer the dock**

105　**Power astern**

106　**Pivoting round the corner and removing the spring**

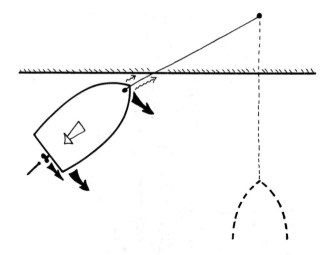

107 Using a head rope to restrain movement backwards

If the boat has to be sprung right round through a full 180° (whether turning ahead or astern), it may be necessary to shift the spring to the far corner of the pontoon partway through the manoeuvre so that she can be swung right round without being hauled alongside the outer end of the pontoon. The operation will be helped by going straight astern as far as possible before snubbing the spring and turning, so keeping the boat well clear of the end of the pontoon as she goes round. If space is limited, her swinging circle can be reduced by moving the lead of the spring forward, as is seen with the boat turning ahead in fig. 101.

Swinging on a Head Rope

This can be useful when you are unable to spring your stern far enough out to proceed as you want. It does require the assistance of the stern's inclination to move in the right direction, but you can see how it works in fig. 107. Wanting to spring out perpendicular with the wall, you find that you can only get out to about 45°. If prop effects haul your stern to starboard on going astern, you can slip the fore-spring and go astern on the head rope. With the head rope preventing her from moving astern, the prop effects will then swing her round as shown, the whole boat pivoting around the point ashore at which the head rope is secured. For moving the boat sideways any distance along the quay, a long head rope should be used and secured well back in from the quayside, as shown.

Further Springing and Warping Manoeuvres

The techniques described so far can be considered as the basics—used for dealing with the most commonly encountered situations. However, the principle of spring-ing, if properly understood, can be employed in an infinite number of guises and variations whenever manoeuvring is required that is too tight to be carried out with engines and rudders alone. The brief selection here is sufficient to give an idea of how to devise your own to suit a particular circumstance.

The lead of a spring line

We have already mentioned the importance of getting the position of this correct, so that the boat will pivot where required. Springing a boat through a very large angle will be facilitated by taking the lead of the spring right round to the outside of stem or stern (fig. 108). It is important to ensure that the hull is protected from chafe by the warp, and that the sterngear (when springing off the bow) is clear of possible damage against the wall.

Checklines

In certain springing situations, usually with a strong stream or wind, it may be necessary to use checklines to prevent her swinging away out of control. In fig. 109 you can see one used to control the stern while springing ahead round a corner using a following stream. The checkline is veered steadily as required throughout the turn, so that the boat is eased round the corner in a controlled manner.

Winding ship

This term describes turning a boat completely end for end in her berth. The wind or stream are used to spring the boat right round, either on a forespring or on a backspring.

108 A spring from the outside

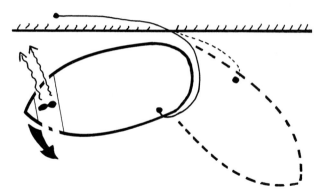

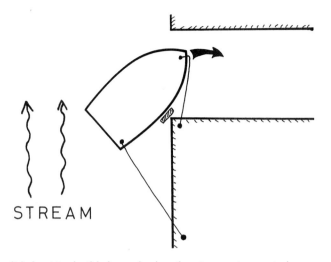

STREAM

109 **A checkline holds the stern against the stream**

It is best to do this by springing the stern out so as to keep the sterngear clear of the wall. Rig a forespring round to the outside of the bow, as described above; then let go all other warps and spring her stern off with a little slipstream to start her swinging. As she goes round use touches astern to keep her bow off the wall. When she is about two-thirds round use slipstream to kick her ahead round into the stream or wind, to slow the swing and lay her alongside the wall. The original forespring now becomes her head rope.

In the absence of convenient wind or stream and the presence of suitable prop effects, the manoeuvre could be started as a conventional springing operation, continued as swinging on the head rope, and finished off with slipstream as above.

Wind or stream can also be used to swing her bow round if you have to, but bear in mind that prop effects in astern may make her difficult to control in the final stages.

Pointing ship

This is a neat little manoeuvre than enables you to swing a boat and position her at any desired angle, whether alongside, anchored, moored to a buoy or between piles. It consists simply of springing her into position then holding her there with a checkline.

To hold the boat at a certain angle when on a mooring (to paint one side in the sun perhaps), you should rig a backspring to the buoy, then simply veer the head rope until stream or wind has swung the boat into the required position (fig. 110). The same can be done at anchor by securing the backspring to the cable and then veering a little cable, thus allowing the bow to pay off downstream while the stern is held by the backspring to the cable. This can be a useful dodge if you are rolling uncomfortably in an anchorage due to a cross-swell, as you can point her round till she is head into the swell. It is important to appreciate, however, that this will cause strong streams and winds to put considerable strain on ground tackle or a mooring.

Perhaps the best use of pointing ship is to reverse your position on a mooring or between piles, if space is tight for turning and you want to proceed the other way on slipping your lines. In this case the pointing process is simply continued until the boat is moored by her stern on the back-spring, the head rope being used as a checkline. The original mooring warp can then be slipped, followed by the original spring when you are ready to leave. If it is practicable to weigh the anchor from aft, the same thing can be done when anchored. If you need to proceed from a mooring at any other angle, you can point ship in the desired direction and slip both warps together before proceeding.

You can reverse either way between piles, pointing the stern or the bow, but the spring will need to be hauled in as she turns in order to keep her clear of the downstream pile: see fig. 94, mentioned in chapter 5. The head rope will have to be slipped, of course, and this can only be done if there is room to lie broadside to the berth. The pointing can be halted at any stage, and both warps slipped to allow the boat to proceed in the required direction.

110 Pointing or sheering

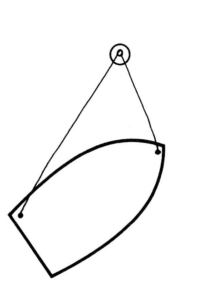

Springing round a pile

There are times when it can be most helpful to spring a boat round a pile (entering or leaving a marina berth, for example), and this is basically the same as springing round a corner. If she is to be swung close round the pile, careful attention must be paid to fendering as she slides along it.

Springing astern round a pile can be a useful method of getting into a tight stern-to berth when wind or stream make a direct sternboard impossible: see fig. 111. The boat should be brought alongside the pile stemming the wind or stream, and secured with forespring and backspring as shown. Then go immediately astern against the backspring before the wind or stream has time to swing your bow in, and the boat will curve round astern into the berth. The stream or wind pressing on the inside of the bow will assist this, and the forespring should be used to control the swing of the bow. Port and starboard stern ropes should then be made fast to the shore and a port head rope to the other pile, as soon as this can be done, and the boat warped back into her berth. You should come astern fairly quickly into the berth to bring the forespring leading as a head rope, where it will more effectively prevent the bow drifting off.

In fig. 112 you can see that there will be little room for a large boat to round up and go astern into one of the piled berths in the foreground, if entering at this state of the tide. She could, however, go alongside the pile then spring astern round it into the berth as described above.

Turning on the bow

A very simple way of turning sharply round in a narrow channel off a quay: turn the boat hard round towards the wall, then push the bow very gently up against it with a

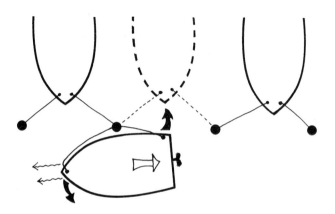

111 **Springing round a pile**

112 Very restricted room to turn: springing round the piling might be the only way in

fender between and go slow ahead with the rudder over. With the wall preventing you from going ahead slipstream, or sometimes the current, will swing the stern round until you can go astern away from it and complete the turn in the channel, using either prop effects astern or a further burst of slipstream ahead. Be careful to come off the wall before turning too far or the bow will lose its grip and slide along it. The same effect can be achieved by running your bow gently aground on a steeply shelving shore and allowing wind or stream to carry the stern round. It is not advisable to motor ahead to turn when aground or you might not get off again!

Clearing from a Raft of Boats

It is very common these days to have to raft up alongside other boats in a berth, whether against a wall or between piles or buoys. Getting away from the inside can be quite tricky, and intelligent use of warps is a great asset.

In order to prevent the outside boats swinging away out of control, it is normal to move out of a raft downstream or downwind so that the outside boats remain lying to their upstream warps during the manoeuvre. If you have the centre boat in fig. 113, you should cast off your lines to the shore and all those to the inside boat except your forespring. The outside boat's forespring and stern rope to you can be cast off, and his stern rope to shore let go from his stern and secured temporarily to the inside boat. This leaves you moored as in fig. 113, and enables you to go slow ahead against your forespring to the inside boat, using rudder and slipstream to swing your stern out.

As you swing, your bow moving in will pull on the outside boat's head rope and backspring, and this will cause him to swing cleanly with you until you reach the position shown in fig. 114. You can now let go all your warps to both boats and go clear astern, leaving the stream to bring the outside boat in alongside the inside one. If there is no-one aboard either of these boats, you must nudge back alongside and send a person over to moor the outside boat up correctly, bearing in mind that his shore lines may need taking in a little. Leave sailing yachts so that their rigging (and especially spreaders) cannot clash if they roll.

If there is any risk of wind preventing the stream from bringing in the outside boat, you should take the end of his stern shore line round your bow and secure it on board

113 Leaving a raft

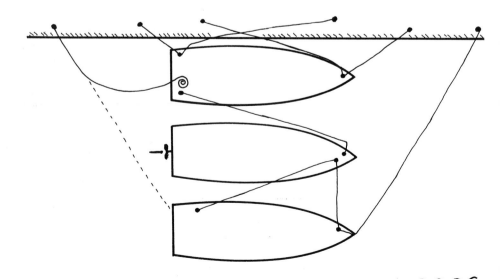

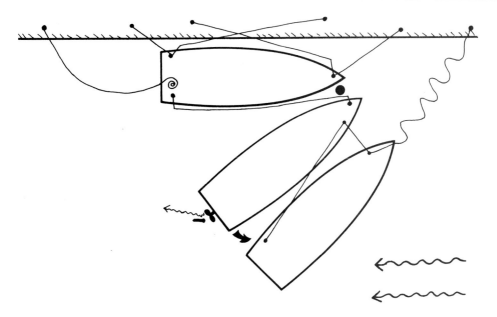

114 Arrangement of lines and opening up a way out

him as you go out. It can then be used to haul in his stern after you are clear.

In a strong stream or wind, it may be advisable to take a checkline ahead to the shore from the outside boat's stern. This can then be veered steadily in order to ease her back alongside. This is particularly useful when clearing from a raft between piles as it enables you to safely spring a long way out to ensure clearing the downstream pile when going astern. Without it the outside boat could swing back in with a real crunch.

Because the boats can drift across the line of the piles (there being no wall to hold them) it may be necessary to give some slack to the outside boat's head rope to prevent it hindering the springing. This problem does not arise when springing off a wall as his shore line will in fact go slack as you spring him round: this should be clear from fig. 113 and 114.

Any such drift along the piles also calls for very careful assessment of your boat's behaviour on going astern, if you are to avoid colliding with the downstream pile on your way out. If avoiding this necessitates springing your stern a long way round, you may find it beneficial to run the forespring round to the opposite side of your stem, as mentioned above. You could also consider the possibility of winching your stern round using the outside boat's checkline. Then go out hard and fast astern, to get clear before wind or stream can carry you onto the downstream pile. Careful fendering will be required against the inside boat throughout this manoeuvre.

The complete operation can also be done the other way

round, so as to come out ahead, but remember the points made earlier in the chapter about the possible difficulties of springing astern. Great care needs to be taken also to keep the outside boat's shore stern line clear of your prop or pushpit as it will slacken when you spring his bow out.

Warping Ship

There will be times when it is not possible to work engines against springs—getting off a lee berth in a strong wind for example—and you will then have to *warp* your boat by hauling her round on ropes. This should be self-explanatory, but bear in mind that the initial warping may well haul her into a position in which you can work her on springs, so think carefully about the leads of warps before starting. Try to arrange the warp so that it can be used for springing when the time comes, rather than having to rig a separate spring and then slip the warp. A boat of any size can exert quite a strong pull just from the pressure of wind and/or stream, so take the lines controlling her round a bollard or ring. It is unwise to just hold the ends directly: she may become too much to hold onto.

7 Narrow Waters Handling

We use the term 'narrow waters' to describe any sort of restricted space, whether it be a narrow canal, shallow river, busy harbour or crowded marina. Much of the information contained in the preceding chapters is, of course, particularly important when negotiating such places, but there are also some specialised techniques and knowledge that you will find useful.

Life at sea, on a well-run ship in fair weather, is a tranquil sort of business, with little to bother anyone other than the ever rolling waves and the odd seagull. If something goes wrong there is usually plenty of time to put on the kettle and brew tea before donning overalls and fixing it.

In narrow waters, however, things are quite different. Even a minor problem can develop very rapidly into a disaster unless instant action is taken, not so much to correct the problem as such but to keep the boat safe while doing so. In the Navy, the 'state of readiness' of a ship is 'shifted up a gear' before entering narrow waters, and you should do exactly the same with your boat.

Preparations for Entering Narrow Waters

There are three main things that you may have to do in a considerable hurry when navigating in narrow waters: anchoring, turning sharply, and mooring up or berthing alongside. Whatever your calculated plans may be, an engine or steering gear breakdown may necessitate rapidly having to anchor to avoid drifting into danger; unexpected obstructions on rounding a bend may cause you to have to turn very sharply and quickly; and a last minute hitch may mean suddenly berthing somewhere other than where you originally planned.

Thus your anchor and windlass should be ready for letting go. All warps and fenders should be on deck in position, but are best not secured until the last moment in case you find you need to berth the other side. A heaving line should be made ready, and a leadline standing by for'ard in case of echo-sounder failure at a crucial moment. You will then be ready to handle most problems.

In order to give yourself maximum thinking time and

manoeuvring space should you get in a tangle, it is sensible to always keep on the windward side of channels when negotiating narrow waters (other traffic permitting). Thinking time can also be reduced if you have a clear idea in your mind at all times of just what you would do and where you could try to go, if certain things went wrong.

Stopping in Emergency

Close to a wall, e.g. when entering a lock, this is best done using a quarter rope as explained in Chapter 4 and one should always be ready when entering restricted locks and docks. In open water, the anchor should be let go and rapidly veered until enough cable is out to reach the bottom; at the same time putting the helm hard over to swing her stern round into the widest space. The anchor should then be allowed to drag at short stay in order to slow the boat and turn her fully head-to-wind or stream, in which position the cable can finally be veered sufficiently to dig in and stop her. This process will prevent her coming up with a jerk that could, in a strong wind or stream, put considerable strains on the gear. If the anchor is on one side of the stem, the boat should be turned before letting it go, to ensure that it runs clear. In a real emergency both anchors should be let go if you have two; otherwise let go the upwind or upstream one so that the boat swings clear of her cable.

If you then find you are anchored in an unsuitable or dangerous place, you can *dredge* downstream by hauling in cable until the anchor begins to drag. By adjusting the length of anchor cable you can control the rate of dragging to enable you to steer with the rudder. If she drags much more slowly than the stream is running, the water flow past her rudder will give you steerage, and you can sheer the boat one way or the other by this means (fig. 115). This will enable you to move across the stream and out of a busy channel, where you can then let out more cable to stop and sort yourself out.

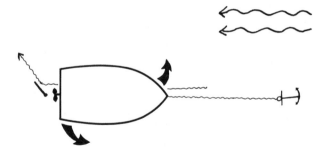

115 Dredging across the stream

Berthing in a Hurry

If you suddenly have to get alongside quickly—perhaps to move out of the way of a large vessel taking up the whole channel—and particularly if you only intend staying there briefly, it is generally a mistake to hurriedly attempt to get all the correct warps across and made fast. Tangles and confusion inevitably result, and all too often it is time to leave again before you have them all secured properly.

A quick and simple way of securing alongside temporarily is to put across a short for'ard or after breast rope as in fig. 66, Chapter 4, depending on whether the wind or stream is from ahead or astern. A boat should not, however, be left unattended like this (fig. 116). If an offshore breeze threatens to blow you away from the wall you would be better to motor slowly ahead against a turning spring until you can leave.

Turning in a Narrow Channel

If wind or stream threaten to carry you a long way during a basic tight turn as described in Chapter 2, there are some special methods to reduce the drift. Let us consider two common situations: turning away from wind and/or stream, and turning into them.

116 A short breast rope holds the boat in against her fenders

Turning away from wind or stream

Turning sharply off the wind can be accomplished fairly easily using a basic technique from Chapter 2 (depending on prop and steering configuration) in conjunction with the effects of the wind as described in Chapter 3. Make the three-point turn so that the sternboard is assisted by the draw of the wind.

Turning sharply away from a stream without being carried too far can be accomplished by utilising the fact that streams are usually much weaker close to the banks than they are in the middle of the channel. Move over close to one bank and kick the stern in with the slipstream, as for a normal three-point turn. The bow will then swing out into the stronger stream and be carried downstream more rapidly than the stern. As she drifts, use astern power and its accompanying prop effects both to keep the stern in the weaker stream and to pull it round upstream (fig. 117).

Before picking your spot to nose out of the stream, check to see that it really *is* weaker at the edge of the water. Sometimes, as on sharp bends or where the water is channelled between steep banks or walls and there may not be any shallows to slow it down, this is not the case. You will also have to contend with the risk of grounding or touching something sticking out of the bottom, with this method. Odd rough patches or patterns of ripples may tell you that there is something to watch out for, under the surface.

Turning towards wind or stream

This is usually best done using the anchor to hold her head into stream or wind, so enabling the stern to swing

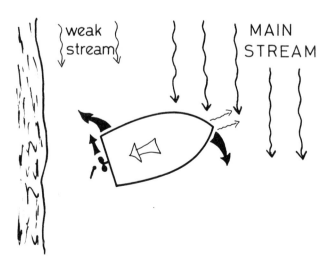

weak stream   MAIN STREAM

117 **Turning away from the stream**

away rapidly with the minimum of sideways drift or forward movement. The basic technique is very similar to stopping in emergency, but rather more controlled.

When turning into a stream, use is made of the variation in strength of flow as described above. You should turn against prop effects and move in close to the bank ahead of you, going hard astern to stop her when the bow is well into the weak part of the stream. Prop effects astern, in conjunction with the stronger stream acting on the stern, will pull it round away from the stream. When she has stopped you should let go the upstream anchor at short stay so that it will drag just enough to virtually halt the drift of the bow. The strong stream will then carry the stern right round until the boat is heading upstream, when you can weigh the anchor and proceed (see fig. 118).

The technique will work just the same if you cannot close the bank and put your bow in the weak stream, but the boat will drift durther downstream during the process. This is an excellent way of turning tightly round in a narrow harbour before berthing, if you enter on the flood. If you judge it well you should be able to turn and slither across into the berth all in one movement. If you turn too soon you can dredge back. As the anchor does not dig in during the manoeuvre, it is quite easy to haul in and recover when berthed (unless it has snagged a bottom chain).

To turn into the wind you should go hard astern until all movement over the ground has ceased, during which time the draw of the wind on her stern will keep her straight. Then give a very brief kick ahead with full helm to start her swinging the way you want her to go, and let go the weather anchor at short stay as described above. She will swing quickly round the anchor, and you can weigh it and

118 **Turning into the stream**

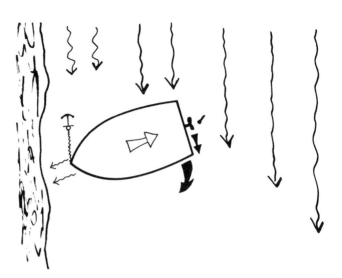

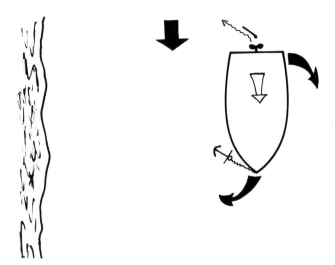

119 Turning into the wind

proceed when she is pointing in the right direction (fig. 119). Note the essential differences between these manoeuvres, depending whether wind or stream is the controlling factor.

Rounding a tight bend

An anchor can be used in similar fashion for assisting a large yacht round a very tight and narrow bend. By letting it go at short stay on beginning the turn, you can use its drag to haul the bow hard in round the bend. This is best done by letting go a kedge off the inner bow as shown in fig. 120; if the lead is one-third of her length back from the bow, it will enable the boat to swing very easily round and give full control of her angle. A light kedge can be easily recovered without affecting the boat's steady movement round the bend, although it is essential to keep it dragging at very short stay (on a short length of cable). If the anchor bites you will find yourself in a little bother!

Turning before leaving a berth

There may be occasions when a large boat cannot with ease proceed from a berth (whether alongside or anchored) without first turning round. Turning in an alongside berth was dealt with in Chapter 6, as was turning at anchor or on a mooring buoy by pointing ship. The latter, however, will not always be convenient, particularly when anchored, and a simpler method of turning will often be more practical.

Having first brought the cable in to short stay (but not short enough to cause the anchor to drag), give the boat a little sheer with a touch of slipstream in order to make

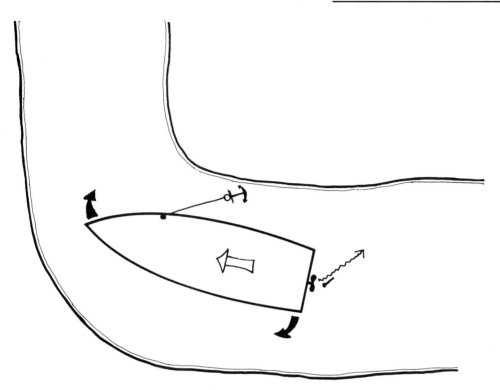

120 Negotiating a very tight bend

the cable lead out to one side of the bow. This should be done against prop effects, so that you can then motor slowly ahead to bring the cable growing aft along that side, before turning her hard the other way round the cable, with slipstream assisted by prop effects, until she is pointing in the desired direction. Then quickly weigh anchor and proceed before she has time to drift back again (fig. 121).

Using bow thrust

This should be fairly obvious. Clearly it can be used to manoeuvre the bow as required, thus allowing you to dispense with working the anchor in all these turning

121 Turning before weighing anchor

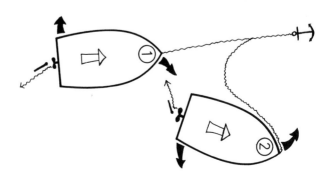

manoeuvres. It must not, however, tempt you into not bothering to prepare the anchor for letting go when the boat is in narrow waters.

Special Handling Problems

There are three special factors that can cause handling difficulties in narrow waters, particularly with relatively large displacement vessels. All are caused by the amount of water pushed out sideways as the hull forges along in the water: in effect, the bow and stern waves. Where space is very restricted these waves cannot simply flow away and gradually disperse as they do at sea, so they build up pressure between the boat and the restriction. (Even in open water you can see the waves built up by the small motor cruiser in fig. 122.) There are three types of restriction that can cause this build-up of pressure: the banks of narrow canals, the bottom in very shallow water, and the hulls of large vessels passing or being passed close to.

122 **A trough forms between the bow and stern waves**

Canal Effect

The bow and stern waves are forced by the close banks of a narrow channel to push out ahead and astern of the vessel: this causes a trough to form amidships and corresponding waves to build up ahead and astern. In a bad case the two waves and the trough between them are clearly visible, and water can be seen draining away from the banks on the approach of the trough.

The faster the boat goes the more rapidly these waves develop and excessive speed is the cause of canal effect. As the effect builds up, steering becomes gradually lighter and less positive, and finally quite ineffective. By this time she is firmly held by the pressure at her bows and suction between her sides and the banks of the canal.

If she then moves over towards one bank the increased pressure on the bow nearest the bank can force her head suddenly and very sharply across into the farther bank. It will be quite impossible to control this sheer with the rudder, although a very experienced skipper might be able, if propeller effects serve, to straighten her up by going hard astern (fig. 123). Dangerous yawing, if not actually striking the bank, can result. This sheer, even when canal effect is slight, can often serve to help push the bow away from a bank and round a corner, almost like a bow thruster. It is,

123 Pressure differences along a hull

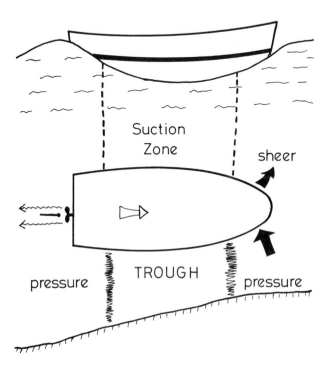

Suction Zone

sheer

TROUGH

pressure   pressure

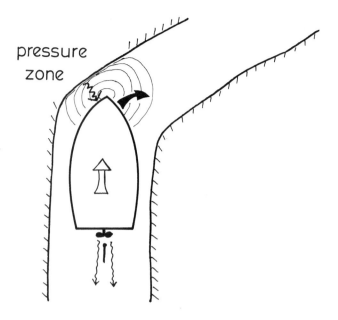

pressure
zone

124 **Sheering round a bend**

however, rather less controllable (fig. 124).

The cure for canal effect is to reduce the speed while in the centre of the channel, until all signs of waves and troughs disappear; the reduction must be gradual as any sudden change in the steady progress of the boat can set off a sheer. You should at all times in a canal keep a sharp eye open for signs of waves building up ahead or astern of the boat, and reduce speed immediately—but gradually—if they do.

Shallow water effect or 'squat'

In water that is less than $1\frac{1}{2}$ times the vessel's draft, similar problems can occur due to the sea bed restricting the movement of the lower parts of the bow and stern waves (see Chapter 9). Excessive speed causes, in particular, the stern wave to build up much higher than normal. This creates a deeper trough ahead of it in which the vessel sits, thus making her squat down at the stern and possibly even touch the ground aft. As the propeller gets closer to the bottom so its slipstream is restricted, causing turbulence and loss of steering control.

On detecting an increase in the height of the stern wave, you should immediately slow down—gradually—until it resumes its normal size. In canals or channels that are both shallow and narrow, these effects can occur together, exaggerating the loss of steering control and increasing the risk of a serious sheer if the stern grounds. On approaching a shallow bank from open water, the bow wave preceding the boat will often build up sufficient pressure against the bottom in the shallows to cause the boat to sheer away from them. The boat is then said to be *smelling the ground*, and a wise skipper will take the hint.

Turbulence of the propeller slipstream can also occur in very shallow water even when a boat is stationary, if too much power is applied to propellers—when turning, for example. This can reduce considerably the effectiveness of the slipstream over the rudder. With twin screws, excessive power ahead and astern on the props when turning hard round in very shallow water can cause sufficient turbulence to almost prevent her turning at all.

Overtaking effect

In this instance the restriction to the flow of bow and stern waves is caused by the close proximity of a large ship passing you. If she approaches from ahead, the bow waves meeting will cause the two bows to sheer away from each other. Because of this it is generally best to pass fairly close to another ship in a narrow canal, knowing that you will sheer away from her; although care needs to be taken that the stern will not then sheer away as it meets her bow wave and the bow be sucked towards her in the trough amidships. If you move across too close to the bank to give her room, canal effect could sheer your bow back out towards her, and her canal effect may drain sufficient water from the banks to cause you to ground. A careful balance needs to be maintained between these two risks, and slow speed is a great asset.

When a vessel is overtaking very close to another, however, things are rather different. The initial interaction is a more gradual one between a bow wave and a stern wave, which will not have the same sheering effect as two bow waves meeting. Shortly after this, however, the smaller boat will find herself in the deep trough beside the large one and this will exert a powerful suction effect that could drag the small boat sharply towards the big one (fig. 125).

If a large ship is making to overtake you very closely in

125 Interaction when passing

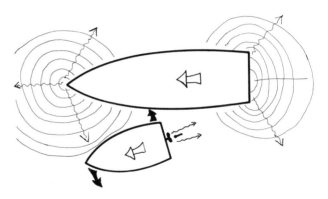

a narrow waterway, you should gradually move over to the bank and reduce speed until she is well past. Your speed should be reduced sufficiently to avoid any canal effect building up between you and the bank, which could sheer you across the channel and under her bow. Watch also for the possibility of the sudden reduction in depth described above.

Passing through Locks

There are certain aspects of boathandling that need to be considered rather carefully when working through locks. The first is the business of manoeuvring in a very restricted space, often crammed full with other boats; the second is that an experienced skipper can employ certain special techniques in order to save himself a great deal of time and effort, particularly when negotiating a long sequence of locks with a small crew.

Basic techniques

The general problem when entering and berthing in a lock is that space rarely permits a technically correct approach for the circumstances—using propeller effects, compensating for wind, etc: see the crowded lock in fig. 126. Usually you will be obliged to approach at a very

126 **Little room to manoeuvre**

shallow angle, and the presence of boats on the opposite wall makes it imperative that you do not allow your stern to swing out or the boat to blow across. Thus you need to stop virtually in a straight line, with just a very slight swing of the stern towards your wall, and very close to it. Given the choice, you should take the windward side, as it makes getting away again much easier: you can simply slip the warps and blow clear.

Stopping in a straight line will present little difficulty to boats with twin screws or swivelling props, but a cross-wind could cause any boat to end up too far off a weather wall. In such a situation recourse must be made to spring-ing, as described in Chapter 6. If your boat is large you cannot afford to have her blow down onto smaller craft that may be berthed on the leeward wall. The priority must be to get a suitable warp ashore as soon as the bow enters the lock, so that it can be secured in time for any necessary springing operation.

Berthing in a single-screw boat with strong prop effects can be quite tricky in a crowded lock. A very slow approach needs to be made, so that prop effects are kept to a minimum by stopping the boat with only a brief touch astern. If the swing of the stern is away from the wall, you should stop just before reaching the berth so that a kick ahead with the rudder over in the slipstream can be used to push her stern across to the wall. The shallow approach angle will prevent you doing this on the way in, as you would when normally berthing with prop effects astern hindering the swing.

If space is very restricted or you are some way off the wall, you should consider making this kick ahead against a turning forespring. This will reduce the distance the boat moves ahead during the operation and also bring her in sideways. An alternative is to pass a quarter rope ashore as soon as possible, and surge this round a bollard in order to stop her and bring her in. If she takes a long time to stop, a quarter rope is essential if you are not to find the lock keeper, fed up with waiting on your very slow approach, closing the gates in your face!

With a boat of any size, whatever her propeller con-figuration, it is seamanlike to have such a warp rigged at all times when a failure to stop in precisely the right place could cause trouble. Entering a lock with a strong following wind and/or stream would be just such a situation. Having stopped the boat in the correct position using one of these warps, she can be kept there by judicious use of throttle and rudder until proper head and stern ropes can be secured ashore.

Although you are unlikely to encounter unpredictable currents when working through locks, other than cross-currents when entering a sea lock (see Chapter 3, fig. 56), there are movements of water to be guarded against. When gates are first opened for you to leave, there is invariably an inward rush of water for a few moments before the levels equalise exactly. If you are to avoid having your bow carried across to the other wall, you should wait until the visible swirl of water ceases before moving off.

A ship in a lock will often leave her propeller turning ahead with the rudder over, to hold herself against the wall. This will produce a strong wash out from her stern, and you must allow for this sweeping you across to the opposite wall. This can be quite tricky if space is tight, as it will first push your bow across, and then your stern, as you pass it. Keep your speed right down on entering, so that you give yourself room and power to kick ahead as required in order to straighten up. And use plenty of fat fenders!

Special techniques

As you gain experience in working through locks, you will doubtless develop your own dodges for speeding up and simplifying the operation. Let me, however, describe a few that I have found useful over the years, particularly when short-handed. Working through locks can be very labour-intensive and often poses problems for a two-man crew handling a fairly large boat.

Probably the most immediate difficulty is getting warps ashore when locking up, as you cannot always be sure of finding some helpful soul waiting at the top of that great unclimbable cliff as you arrive. In a crowded lock, or with a following wind, you cannot wait about for someone to turn up. Your ally here is the quarter rope. With that secured ashore, you can then hold her alongside using engine and rudder, and take your time securing properly.

If there is one crew ashore, send him this warp first and ensure that he makes it fast right at the back of the lock so that you have room to go ahead on it and draw the boat in alongside. If there is no-one there on your arrival, put your bow against the jetty outside and send your crew over to make it fast. With rudder and prop holding the boat along-side on this warp, you can amble up for'ard and give him the head rope. You can save the bother of a stern rope by putting a stopper round the quarter rope, as shown in fig. 127, which you can heave in to make it lead to the stern while the boat rises or falls in the lock. You should stop the prop so as to give slack on the quarter rope, and use a very slippery line for the stopper in order to reduce friction as it slides round the main warp.

If you are working through a long flight of locks, much effort can be saved by leaving a person or two ashore to simply walk from lock to lock with the ends of the warps. If given sufficient slack, one crew can take both warps,

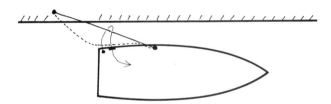

127 Using the quarter rope as a stern line

dropping the stern line over a suitable bollard in the next lock as he passes. With the stern rope rigged from the quarter as described in the previous paragraph, two people working this way can move the largest of vessels through a flight of locks with ease. A heaving line with a bucket on the end can be used to pass mugs of tea up to the walker!

When locking down there will be no great swirl of water in the lock, and it is sometimes quite feasible for a large boat to simply float in the middle of an empty lock without the bother of using warps at all. This can save huge amounts of time when working short-handed through locks that you have to operate yourself. The crew ashore can simply run along opening and closing gates and sluices as required, while the skipper steams quietly from lock to lock stopping in the middle of each one.

One short-cut you should never take, however, is to leave the boat unattended even for a moment, particularly when locking down.

Risk of Collison

Clearly this is greater in narrow waters than it is at sea, and more thought needs to be given to collision avoidance than a mere slavish adherence to the Collision Regulations— other than perhaps Rules 1 and 2, which I recommend you digest thoroughly. It is important to appreciate the lack of manoeuvrability of very large vessels in narrow waters, and it should be clear from Chapters 1, 2 and 3 just what the consequences can be of a large single-screw merchantman having to go full astern to avoid another boat. Any vessel motoring with a stream has considerably less control over her movements than one stemming it, so she should always be given right of way, especially through narrow gaps such as bridge arches where the stream will be running even more strongly than elsewhere.

Keep to the right-hand side of channels, in general. Staying right out of the channel altogether (depth permitting) enables a small boat to avoid all contact with big vessels. In a foul stream it can also enable a low-powered craft to make headway, where she might be unable to motor over the full strength of stream in the centre of the channel.

Crossing big-ship or ferry channels should be done as though they were shipping lanes: rapidly and at right angles. Use, and listen for, manoeuvring and overtaking sound signals which can give warning of unexpected intentions:

One short blast	I am altering course to starboard
Two short blasts	I am altering course to port
Three short blasts	My engines are going astern
Five or more blasts	Are you taking enough avoiding action, *or* Wake up!
Two long, one short	I intend overtaking on your starboard side
Two long, two short	I intend overtaking on your port side
Long, short, long, short	You may overtake as signalled
One prolonged blast	Sound on approaching a blind bend

8 Stability and Sails

This may seem a strange subject for a chapter in a book like this, but before we can go on to discuss the handling of a boat under power at sea, it will be found helpful to understand the basic principles of stability in the water, particularly when rolled about by waves. The effects that waves have on a boat, and the possible risk of their capsizing or overwhelming her, should then be easier to visualise.

The capacity of a boat to stand up to the pressure of wind on her sails without falling over is even more closely related to her inherent stability. As we shall see, sails can often be very useful to a boat under power, be she an auxiliary sailing yacht or a motor vessel, so it is rather important that you understand how they will affect her stability before you gaily haul acres of canvas up your mast. The substantial superstructures found on many power cruisers are also wind-catchers, as well as topside weight, as owners of pure power cruisers should remember.

Designed Stability

Boats are designed with certain stability factors that cause them to return to the upright position when they are heeled over, and there is a maximum angle of heel at which these factors will operate. Beyond this angle there will be no righting force and the vessel will continue to roll over until she reaches a stable position, which is generally when she is upside-down.

In fig. 128 you can see how this works. The weight of a

128 Centres of gravity and buoyancy

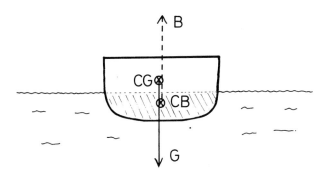

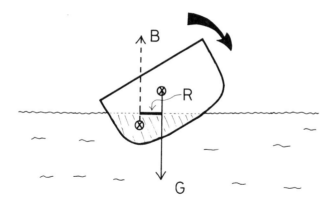

129   **Righting lever**

boat can be said to be concentrated at a point called the *centre of gravity* (CG) and exerts a downward force (G) as shown by the arrow. This is counteracted by the hull's buoyancy (B) pushing upwards and the boat remains stable and at rest, neither sinking down into the water nor floating up into the air. Buoyancy can also be said to concentrate its efforts at a single point, the *centre of buoyancy* (CB), and when the boat is upright the CG and CB lie vertically in line.

If a boat is heeled over in calm water one side of the hull is forced down into the water and the other side lifted out of it. This causes the upward force of buoyancy to move across to the immersed side, away from the centre of gravity, so creating a *righting lever* (R) between the two forces (fig. 129). With the weight of the boat acting downwards at one end of R and the buoyancy of the immersed hull acting upwards at the other end, we have a powerful force turning the boat back into an upright position. The wider the beam, the further out the buoyancy can move and the greater will be the righting tendency. As the boat then comes upright, so the centre of buoyancy gradually moves back to its original position, vertically in line with the centre of gravity, and the boat becomes stable again.

Thus we can see that when a boat first heels, the CB moves away from the CG and the righting moment increases steadily. At a certain angle, however (as the movement of the centre of buoyancy slows down), this righting force will reach a maximum, after which any increase in heel will cause the line through which the CG acts to start closing with the CB, reducing the distance between them and so the righting moment.

With a further continuation in heel, a point will be reached at which these two forces coincide, whereupon there will be no righting lever and no righting force. Beyond this *capsizing angle* the centre of gravity will act outboard of the centre of buoyancy, thus causing the boat to capsize (fig. 130).

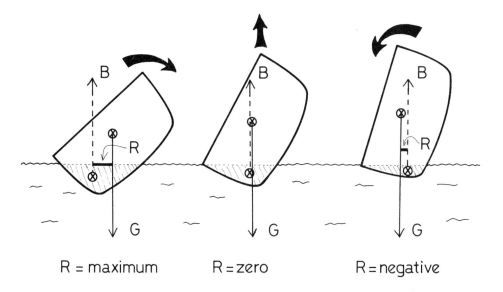

R = maximum   R = zero   R = negative

130 **Capsizing**

131 **Righting effect of deep keel**

The values of both the *maximum righting angle* and the capsizing angle depend largely on the relative positions of the buoyancy force and the gravity force. It should be apparent from a comparison of figs 130 and 131 that a shallow-draft motor boat with relatively high CG will have considerably smaller values of both than a sailing yacht with a deep, heavy keel. The motor boat will likely have a maximum righting angle of around 45° and a capsizing angle of about 85°, beyond which she will continue turning over until completely upside down where she will remain, being extremely stable.

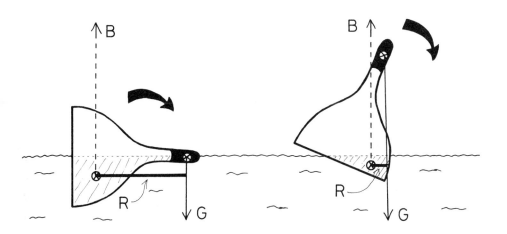

R = maximum   R = positive

The deep-keel yacht, on the other hand, will have her maximum righting force when hove right down to 90° and will maintain a righting force all the way round to virtually 180°, in which position she will, unless of great beam (multihulls) or in very calm water, be so unstable as to return upright anyway. The strong buoyancy created by wide beam works just as efficiently when a boat is upside down as when she is upright. A narrow yacht with deep ballast keel requires very little heel when upside down for her gravity to move outside her buoyancy, and thus exert a rapidly increasing force to bring her upright.

Clearly, these latter qualities are most desirable in a boat that may well be flung right on her beam ends by a ferocious squall of wind. A power boat, not having to withstand wind pressure on large sails, does not need this amount of ultimate stability. Nor, as we shall see, does she want it.

Stability in Waves

In a seaway this simple stability picture is confused by the fact that it is the waves themselves that cause a boat to heel over, by first lifting one bilge, then passing under the hull and lifting the other. This causes the boat to roll from side to side, and the centre of buoyancy, instead of pushing neatly and steadily up on the lower bilge as in fig. 129, roams about, its position depending on the shape of the immersed part of the hull. The result can be seen quite clearly in fig. 132. A narrow, deep-keeled yacht with slack bilges will remain almost upright when rising beam-on to a wave, there being little buoyancy pushing up on her

132 **Hull shape and heeling from waves**

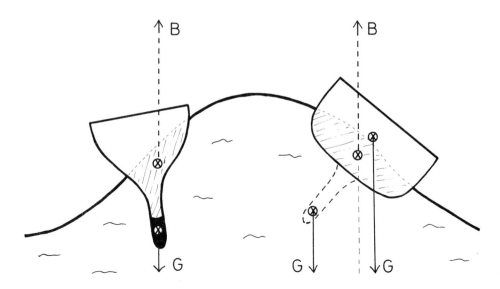

higher bilge compared with the considerable weight of her keel pulling down on it.

The beamy vessel with full bilges and little depth of keel, on the other hand, will sit almost level with the face of the wave as the buoyancy of her upper bilge is considerable, and the high CG exerts a much smaller righting moment than would a deep ballast keel (the broken outline). With the hull symmetrically immersed in the water the CB will not move at all; and if the CG is above it as shown here and in fig. 128, the boat will capsize. The righting power of wide bilges does not exist in this situation, so the stability of the boat must be produced by ensuring that at all times the CG is below the CB, in spite of the apparent efficiency shown in fig. 128, where they are the other way round.

It should be apparent that a beamy boat with shallow draft and full bilges will roll further—and thus be more easily capsized by a wave—than a deeper keeled hull, whose considerable ultimate stability clearly protects her from capsize by wind or waves. Boats intended for inland waters, whether sail or power, can gain stability from wide beam, but at sea a boat's stability must come basically from a low CG combined with reasonably slack bilges.

Sea-going displacement power craft and sailing yachts will be found generally to have these attributes. Sea-going planing craft possess them to a greater degree than inland planing boats; the deeper Vee shape of their hulls gives them slacker bilges and a lower CG although not nearly as much as in displacement types. The stability of a boat at sea can thus be roughly gauged from how closely her hull resembles those at opposite ends of this design spectrum, as shown in fig. 132. Now let us see why power boats are deliberately designed with less stability than sailing boats.

Period of Roll

The extent of a boat's rolling and her maximum safe angle of heel are not the only considerations in the design of her stability. The rapidity and violence of rolling can affect not only comfort but also the ability to work the boat. Violent rolling puts great strains on a boat and her fittings; heavy objects have been ripped clean from their mountings.

The period of a boat's roll is the time taken for her to go completely from one side to the other and back again. It is a constant factor which does not alter with the *degree* of roll: the heavier the rolling the more violent it tends to be, as the boat attempts to get back to the other side within the same time.

It should be apparent from fig. 132 that the lower the CG the more rapidly the boat will tend to come upright from a roll, and the shorter her rolling period. The shorter the period, the more violently she will roll. In a sailing boat the constant air pressure on her sails steadies her considerably against rolling. She may roll away from a wave as it lifts her weather bilge and reinforces the heeling action of wind on sails, but when she slides down the back of it the wave will have greater difficulty in then rolling her against the wind and the weight of her keel (fig. 133).

A power boat, without the steadying influence of sails, would roll horrendously if she had a centre of gravity as low as that of an offshore sailing yacht. In practice it will be positioned to provide a balance between reasonable motion at sea and stability against capsize, depending on the purpose for which she is designed.

Clearly, a boat that does something she is not designed for in a seaway could indulge in some strange and alarming behaviour. Setting sails on a power boat would reduce her rolling noticeably, but would also create the possibility of a strong wind capsizing her, particularly when reinforced by a wave rolling her to leeward. A sailing boat motoring without sails will roll viciously and even more so if she is dismasted as her CG is further lowered. Any boat that has her CG moved will alter her motion when motoring in waves: becoming either less stable and less violent if it is raised, or more stable and more violent it if is lowered.

With experience, the feel of a boat's rolling period will provide you with a good empirical guide as to her maximum

133 **Righting against wave and wind effect**

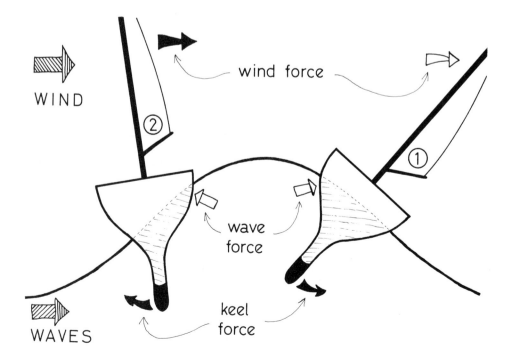

WIND

wind force

② ①

wave
force

keel
force

WAVES

safe angle of heel. Any increase in the height of her CG (see next section) will slow this rolling period, giving you warning of reduced stability. If her rolling is so slowed that she appears reluctant to return from each roll, then stability has been reduced to a dangerous level.

Factors Affecting Stability

Any boat properly designed for going to sea should provide adequate stability in normal conditions; handling abnormal ones will be discussed in Chapter 9. It should be apparent that any major movement of her designed Centre of Gravity upwards or sideways could have very deleterious effects on the stability in even moderate seas. Large numbers of fuel drums, stowed on deck for a long passage, could raise a power boat's CG quite noticeably, reducing her maximum safe angle of heel and slowing her rolling period. In such a situation you should transfer diesel from the drums into the main tanks as often as possible, or the loss of weight from tanks low down could cause the CG to rise even further—perhaps to a dangerous level. An increasing slowness of roll should alert you to what is happening.

Shifting the CG to one side will reduce stability when the boat rolls that way (fig. 129). Although I do not imagine any readers would go to sea with a heavy list to one side, this can gradually happen unnoticed on passage if one of a pair of large wing fuel tanks is run right down while the other remains full. The same thing applies to water tanks and even food stores on a long passage.

Shipping water on the deck of a vessel with solid bulwarks can cause serious instability if freeing ports are not large enough to clear it very quickly, or rubbish or jammed hinges keep them blocked. The rise in CG caused by the weight of water (and a few hundred gallons is a considerable weight) is compounded by the *free surface effect* of the water running down to the lower side when she rolls, thereby moving the CG the wrong way. The most stable of boats can very easily capsize in such circumstances. In fig. 134 you can see how the weight of water on deck moves the CG upwards and across to the lower side as she rolls, sufficient here to convert a positive righting force into a negative capsizing force.

Free surface effect in a large bilge or full-width fuel tank can decrease stability quite noticeably in this way. Large fuel and water tanks should contain baffles to prevent this (fig. 135). Instability is worsened by the momentum built up as the liquid rushes from side to side with each roll (compare with synchronous rolling, Chapter 9).

Large open cockpits and sunken wheelhouses can cause

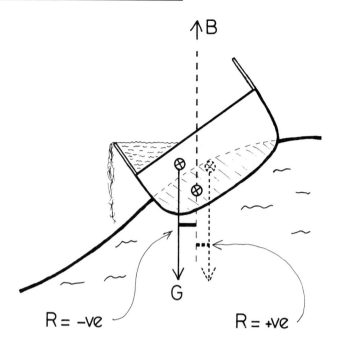

134 **Free surface effect reduces stability**

a dangerous sideways shift of the centre of gravity if they ship quantities of water and the boat is rolling. This can have the effect of reducing a motor boat's capsizing angle fron perhaps 85° to as little as 55° if the cockpit fills with water at that angle. A large wave coming aboard can fill the cockpit with sufficient water to make her capsize on a roll at angles considerably less than her designed safe maximum.

Using Sails

There are three purposes for which sails can be used on a boat that is under power: auxiliary and emergency propulsion, steadying against rolling, and manoeuvring. Although

135 **Baffles to limit free surface effect**

in suitable conditions virtually any boat can use sails for any or all of these purposes, for it to be a practical proposition in normally experienced conditions, a boat must have both lateral stability as discussed above, and directional stability as discussed in Chapters 2 and 3. The precise requirements will vary with the use to which the sails are to be put.

Auxiliary and emergency propulsion

For a boat to stand up to wind pressure on the area of sail necessary to drive her particular type of hull through the water, she must not only have a large maximum safe angle of heel but also a large righting force. Both characteristics can be produced by either a deep and heavy keel or a very wide beam, although the righting force of the latter will be variable and unreliable in a seaway. The easier a boat is to push through the water the less sail will be required; a light, or narrow and fine-lined, boat being driven by much less sail than a heavy or bluff-bowed vessel. The latter type will need more area and thus greater stability.

To make progress forward without blowing excessively to leeward, a boat needs a reasonably deep draft: the greater the sail area, the greater the required draft to counteract the greater sideways force of large sails. (If the sails were only set when going downwind, leeway would be an advantage.)

For a boat to sail in a reasonably straight line without having to carry large amounts of helm, the centre of effort (CE) of her sails must be roughly in the same position along the boat as her centre of lateral resistance (CLR), ideally just abaft it so that she will tend to round up into the wind. This will cause her to spill the wind out of her sails if she is left to her own devices, rather than bear away from the wind with the full strength of it pressing on her sails.

Lightweight planing boats, however large their maximum safe angle of heel or deep the Vee of their hulls, will not sail to any viable or safe degree at all, even if they have masts suitable for setting sail. They do not possess the necessary weight low down to give sufficient righting force; nor the draft to prevent leeway; nor the depth of keel aft to provide the necessary directional stability. They could make use of sails to blow downwind, but even then only if they have rudders to steer with. Such a sail would need to be set right for'ard in order to prevent its thrust continually swinging the boat round her deep forefoot. Even then, the combination of small rudders and deep forefoot would make steering far from easy.

Clearly, sailing yachts and motor-sailers have the necessary characteristics, and so (to a lesser but still useful extent) do many deep-drafted displacement power boats. The traditional fishing boat type, often with two masts, can set a spread of sail along its length such as to balance its overall CE against the CLR of the hull. In reasonable conditions of wind and sea such a boat will sail well downwind and very acceptably across the wind. Her fairly deep draft will keep leeway down to a reasonable level; her long keel and depth aft, combined with a large rudder, will give good directional stability and steering control; and the ballast low down will give her a reasonable righting tendency. The sum of her abilities is unlikely to be good enough for her to sail to windward, however, as doing so requires an efficiency of hull and sailplan that many old-fashioned sailing boats barely have. You can see a good example of such a boat in fig. 136.

This type of boat, together with motor-sailers and auxiliary sailing craft, can very profitably use sails not only for emergency propulson should their engines fail, but also to motor-sail in conjunction with their engines to save fuel, reduce noise and vibration, and give a more comfortable

136 **A comfortable motorsailer which will rely strongly on power**

motion in waves due to the steadying effect of the sails. A very comfortable speed can be maintained with the engine turning much more slowly than would be required under power alone. It is important, however, to think of the engine as an adjunct to the sails, and not the other way round. In this way, the boat enjoys the calm and comfort of moving under sail, and the engine increases the speed achieved out of all proportion to the revolutions set. Motor-sailing also enables a sailing craft to go much closer to the wind than otherwise, an important factor for a small boat trying to get somewhere or flog off a lee shore in a blow.

Engine revolutions should be no more than is necessary to give a healthy improvement in both speed and close-windedness; and the boat should be handled as though she were purely sailing. If engine speed is excessive, or any attempt is made to pinch too close to the wind, she will cease motor-sailing and begin motoring, with an accompanying increase in motion, discomfort and fuel consumption. This may be no hardship to a powerful motor boat intent on getting to windward regardless of discomfort, or even a motor-sailer with a big engine. Both may prefer to motor, and simply use sails for steadying: see next section.

A sailing boat with a low-powered auxiliary and considerable windage, however, will invariably make to windward more efficiently motor-sailing than motoring, even though she may have to make a number of tacks. Not only will her speed under sail and power be much greater than under power alone, but she will move more steadily, at an angle to the waves, than if she tries to bash straight into them with her tiddley little engine and large windage. Lacking the power to drive through and over the waves, she will simply be constantly knocked backwards by them, and spend long periods of time pitching up and down in the same hole. In such a boat it is a great mistake to hand sails and try motoring to windward in anything of a sea.

Steadying sails

Small sails rigged correctly can steady both the lateral rolling under power and also the steering. In the former case, the sail works as explained in fig. 133. A steadying sail does not affect the boat's period of roll (which is a factor of her design), so the smaller angle of roll takes the same time, giving a slower roll as well as a smaller one.

Power boats should set as small a sail as will reduce their rolling to an acceptable level. Too large a sail will cause noticeable leeway in shallow draft boats, and may even heel light ones enough to have a damaging effect on stability. The mizzen on the little motor-sailer in fig. 137 would set a sail quite adequate for steadying her.

If sail is set for steadying purposes only, on a sailing craft, rather than motor-sailing, an area any larger than necessary will merely heel her over and increase discomfort. The short rolling period of a sailing boat necessitates larger steadying sails than are sufficient for an equivalent sized power boat, however. A dismasted sailing boat should make all attempts to get some sail up, in order to counteract the vicious rolling she will experience. A corner of any old sail hoisted up some sort of jury mast will improve her motion considerably. In fig 138 you can see a steadying sail rigged on an old pilot cutter on passage under engine. Look at the horizon and think how she would roll without it!

Ideally, you should be able to site a steadying sail in various places along a boat, depending on conditions. By moving it about in relation to the CLR, a turning moment can be created that may profitably improve any difficulties you are having with steering. If the boat is tending to gripe round into the wind, setting the sail for'ard will counteract this by pushing her head downwind. If she has a tendency

137 The mizzen is likely to be more effective as a steadying sail than for propulsion

138 Steadying sail, smaller than the mainsail, in a rough sea

to run off the wind, the sail should be set aft, in the style of the traditional fishing boat mizzen, to turn her head into the wind. Otherwise it should be set amidships where it will least affect the steering. The little boat in fig. 137 can set varying amounts of sail along her length, enabling her to do all these things, and also motor-sail. The motor vessel in fig. 139, however, could set only a small steadying sail on her mast amidships.

Manoeuvring with sails

This ability of sails to create turning effect round the CLR can often be used to assist manoeuvring, as well as steering straight. A sail right for'ard, especially if hauled over to weather to kill its drive, can make a bow blow off downwind very rapidly indeed. This can be a useful ploy for getting clear of a berth or turning hard round to avoid an obstruction, and if the sail is hoisted quickly enough it will often turn the bow more quickly than can be done with power alone. Springing the bow out of a berth can be a slow process if prop effects are not strongly in favour, and if the boat herself is sheltered by the quay from a handy offshore wind the heads'l can sometimes be hoisted high enough to catch the wind and blow her bow off (fig. 140).

Conversely, a mizzen can be used to swing the stern downwind and thus help to keep her head up into the wind. This is especially helpful to low-powered auxiliaries with much windage of rigging for'ard, or launches with

139 A steadying sail would be amidships

140 Backed sail to push bow out

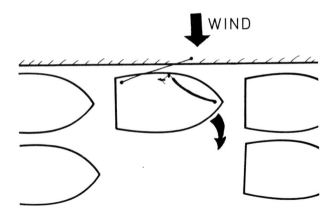

141 Boat A sets her mizzen on the mooring, and swings round against the stream to lie head to wind in more comfort. Boat B suddenly realizes that the wind is blowing her bow off towards A and she has insufficient power to turn up into it. She can either set a mizzen to help her round to position (1) and safety, or set a backed headsail and bear away sharply to (2). A low-powered auxiliary, she lacks the power either to round up into the wind before the stream sets her onto A, or to go astern against the stream.

for'ard wheelhouses, both of which can experience great difficulty turning into the wind. It can also be set while at anchor, or swinging to a buoy, to keep the boat head-to-wind if a stream is holding her beam-on to a bit of a swell, causing her to roll badly. Even if it does not turn her completely into the wind, it will swing her round to a better position and also steady the rolling. As with a heads'l, a mizzen should be sheeted in as tightly as possible for this, even hauled to weather if you can, to maximise the swing-ing effect and minimise forward drive (fig. 141).

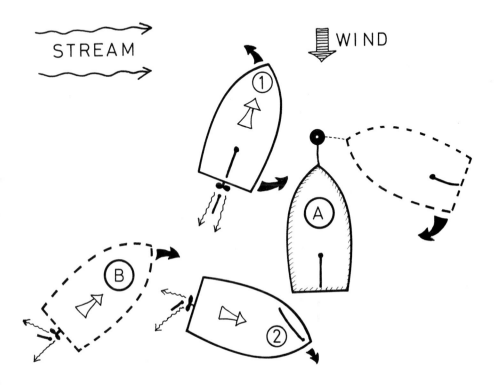

The Thames Barge anchored on the right of fig. 142 has her mizzen set to hold her into the wind. These mizzens are too small for serious sailing purposes and have evolved as part of the rig solely to improve manoeuvring. They very cleverly sheet down to the rudder so that when turning into the wind they are automatically hauled aback to push the stern round. Originally for helping the vessels to tack, they are much used by modern barge skippers for assisting in turning upwind under power against the colossal windage for'ard of all those spars, sails and rigging.

If your boat is equipped with sails, it is good seamanship to have them ready for use in narrow waters (covers off and sheets in place), both to assist turning and provide propulsion in case of engine breakdown (see Chapter 11).

142 **Barge mizzens (right), one set and one brailed up: at the extreme end of the hull, they help turning**

9 Handling at Sea

In calm water there is no difference between handling a boat under power at sea or anywhere else, except that there is a lot more room. If there are waves of any size, however, then you should understand the effects they will have on your boat, and the way you must handle her in order to prevent them capsizing you, sinking you, damaging you or discomforting you; this last being perhaps rather more important than it sounds. The dangers inherent in capsizing, sinking and sustaining damage need no elaboration; the dangers inherent in grave discomfort are rather more subtle, but no less real. The discomfort that can be experienced when motoring in a rough sea is hard to describe to someone who has not experienced it: it can drain a person of all energy and will-power at just the time when they are needed most. It can wreck the capacity to make rational and seamanlike decisions in just the sort of situation in which life could depend on doing so.

The Behaviour of a Boat in Waves

There are three basic motions that a boat experiences when motoring in a seaway: rolling, pitching and yawing. Each has its own cause, and creates its own problems. Before we explain them, let us consider just what a wave is: then the behaviour of a boat in a sea full of them should be easier to understand.

Waves are not moving lumps of water but moving chunks of energy, generally caused by the wind; the passage of each chunk causing a lump of water to lift up and then down again, creating a wave. At the same time, the passage of the energy causes the water in the wave to circle round, flowing forward at the top and back again at the bottom (fig. 143). This draws water from the trough, creating a backward flow there which is of some importance to us.

As the wind is never regular, neither are the waves. A normal seaway contains many different trains of waves, running in slightly different directions and at slightly different heights. When waves coincide they produce one wave as high as the sum of all their heights; when troughs coincide they produce a trough with the combined depth

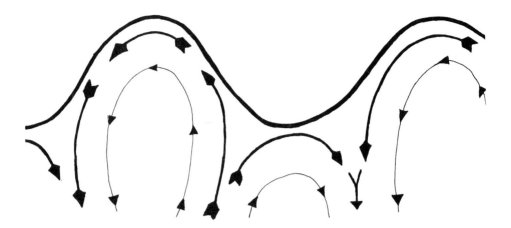

of all of them; and when a wave coincides with a trough it produces a flat patch. Most of the time the waves just vary a bit in height and direction but now and again a big one comes along, or a calm patch, or a deep hole in the water. That these variations will come along must be borne in mind when considering the behaviour of a boat in waves.

143 Movement within waves

Rolling

This is caused by waves picking up one bilge, then rolling on under the boat to drop the bilge and pick up the other one. The weather bilge then slides into the following trough and is picked up by the next wave: and so it goes on. It is greatest when motoring beam-on to the waves as the buoyancy of the complete length of the bilge is exposed to the full lifting power of the wave. A round-bilge hull rolls more readily than one with hard chines, the flat area and buoyancy of the latter being more difficult to push down into the water. The rolling of a round-bilge hull can be reduced by bilge keels, their flat areas presenting great resistance to the water as the bilge goes down.

The moment the boat starts rolling, she automatically rolls back and forth in accordance with the time of her natural period of roll. This will cause her to sometimes roll against the next wave, sometimes with it, and usually just altogether out of step with the arrival of the waves. The result is that rolling is both uneven and irregular: at times she will roll heavily (when her natural roll coincides with that caused by the wave), and at others hardly at all (when her roll opposes that caused by the wave).

If, however, her rolling period is very similar to the time between encountering each wave, this irregularity will diminish, possibly to the point at which every natural roll is reinforced by the roll from a passing wave. Her rolling will then become very even and regular, each roll growing steadily heavier as it is progressively accentuated by a wave. Eventually the roll will exceed the maximum designed limit of the boat, and she will capsize. This is known as *synchronous rolling*. It is rarely encountered in small boats, and virtually impossible in sailing vessels under power, for the simple reason that by the time the waves are big enough to roll the boat noticeably, their period of encounter is normally far longer than the rolling period of such boats. It can, however, occur when the period of encounter is an exact multiple of the period of roll (twice, three times as long), although the intervening non-synchronous rolls will tend to reduce its effect. It is most likely to occur when the waves are abeam.

Pitching

This occurs when a boat is motoring into the waves, each wave first picking up the bow, then dropping it and picking up the stern. As with rolling, a lack of synchronisation between the period of encounter of the waves and the natural period of pitching of the boat normally causes it to be irregular. Although it does not have the dangers that rolling has, violent pitching in a short sea can put great stresses on the boat and her crew.

In suitable conditions synchronous pitching can occur in the same way as its rolling counterpart and the result is an increasingly violent and regular motion. It is more likely to be experienced than synchronous rolling as head seas have a much shorter period of encounter than beam seas. Its likelihood decreases rapidly as course is altered away from a direct head sea.

Boats with full bows will pitch more than those with a lean entry, due to their buoyancy and shape making the waves lift them more readily. They will also crash down violently onto the surface of the trough, where a boat with a fine bow will sink relatively gently through it: see figs 144 and 145. The fine bow must have increasing flare towards deck level in order to prevent it disappearing under altogether, and also to keep spray down. Boats with short ballast keels will pitch more than those with long keels, due to the 'see-sawing' effect of the ballast, concentrated low amidships, acting like a pendulum (fig. 146). This gives the short-keeled yacht a shorter pitching period than a long-keeled one, and makes her more prone to synchronous pitching.

Yawing

When a boat is motoring in a following sea, each wave picks up the stern, then drops it and picks up the bow. In theory it is similar to pitching but in reverse, and rather

144   A full bow with a
very rounded form and
considerable overhang.
Dutch barges were
designed to suit the shape
and length of waves in
their particular waters

145   A fairly vertical
stem, but moderately
flaring sides typical of the
traditional motor cruiser

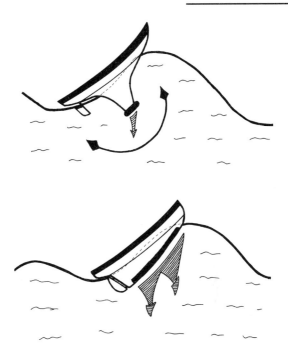

146 **Keel length and pitching**

gentler due to the boat motoring away from the waves rather than into them, thus lengthening considerably their period of encounter. It is, however, complicated by the forward-moving water at the crest of the wave, which tends to carry the stern of the boat bodily forward as it lifts it. At the same time the bow, stuck in the reverse water flow of the preceding trough (or the back of the preceding wave), is unable to move forward, so each wave tries to pivot the stern around the bow and swing the boat beam-on to the seas (fig. 147). As the wave passes under the boat, so the

147 **Broaching forces**

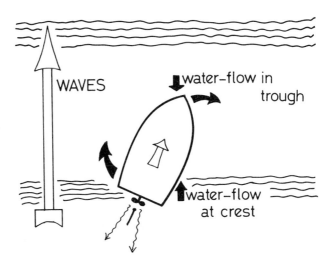

WAVES

water-flow in
trough

water-flow
at crest

stern drops into the following trough and the bow is picked up by the crest. She then tends to straighten out her course, her bow now being carried forward by the crest and her stern dragged back by the trough.

This effect is most noticeable in boats with fine bows that dig easily into the trough or preceding wave, and plump sterns that present great resistance to the moving water at the crest. It is exaggerated by excessive windage aft, the wind then contributing to the tendency of her stern to swing down wind and wave, and excessive draft for'ard preventing her bow from being quickly swung back on course. The effectiveness of rudders will be reduced in the forward moving water at the crest.

A bow with plenty of buoyancy like the one in fig. 144 would be less inclined to bury in a trough than the one in fig. 145; and the cruiser stern of the boat on the left in fig. 148 would present less resistance to the overtaking crests

148 **Cruiser stern (left), and a flat transom on a beamy twin-screw boat**

than would the wide flat transom on the right. The large, deep rudder on the cruiser-sterned boat would give much better steering control in following seas than the small twin rudders that the boat on the right will have. Compare the rudder in fig. 13 with the twins in fig. 29.

The Behaviour of Waves

The basic shape and pattern of waves as described above will only be experienced if there is no interruption to their steady progress. Like streams, their behaviour is greatly affected by obstacles placed in their way. It is important to realise, however, that the shape and pattern of a wave-train will be affected by anything obstructing the passage, not just of the waves themselves, but of the energy driving them. The water circulation in a wave, and the energy driving it, extends to a depth equal to the distance the waves are apart (the wavelength).

If anything causes the lower part of this energy to slow its forward movement, the upper part (in the crest of the wave) will continue at its original speed and thus move faster than the bottom. This causes the front face of the wave to steepen as the crest catches up with the preceding trough; the whole wave to increase in height as this steepening squeezes the water upwards; and the waves to bunch up closer together as they gradually catch up the ones slowing down ahead. If this process continues sufficiently, the shape of the wave will become increasingly unstable, until finally gravity will cause the water at the crest to topple forward down the face of the wave. The wave is then said to break. This should not be confused with water that is merely blown as spray off the crest of a wave by the wind.

Two basic factors can cause a slowing down of the lower part of the wave: shallow water, and a stream running against the direction of movement of the waves. If the depth of water decreases to somewhere approaching the length of the waves, the lower part of the water circulation begins to drag against the bottom and slow down, much as a stream does in shallow water. The effect of a stream opposing the movement of the waves should be apparent. The result of either event is waves that are shorter, steeper, and generally higher than the prevailing sea; and more likely to break.

Clearly, such change in both the shape and length of the waves will have a marked effect on the behaviour of a boat. The steeper sides of the wave will cause her to roll further over, and pitch to a greater angle. Her stern will rise less readily to the steeper wave, and the increased forward-moving water at the crest will cause her to yaw with greater force and momentum. If the crest actually breaks over the boat, the sheer weight of water falling on her could cause structural damage and a serious loss of stability (Chapter 8). The shortening of the wavelength will heighten the risk of both synchronous pitching and rolling.

In contrast to these short, steep waves are the long, smooth ones known as *swell*. They are either fore-runners of very large seas many many miles away to windward, or the dying remains of very large seas that were running in the same place a while ago. With no wind blowing on them, they spread out to become longer, smoother and less steep than normal, giving boats a gentle motion with little risk of discomfort or danger.

The effect on waves of shallow water or strong contrary streams is often sufficient to make a large but otherwise harmless sea extremely uncomfortable or even dangerous. If both shallow water and a strong stream work together the effect on the waves is exaggerated, to the extent that even a long gentle swell can become dangerous. Although shallow water normally reduces the speed of a stream or current, a strong ebb tide running out over a shallow harbour bar can produce precisely these conditions, turning a perfectly manageable sea into a maelstrom in the space of a few yards. Even in a barely noticeable swell from seaward, when conditions on the bar can seem quite placid much of the time, a combination of the rapidly ebbing stream and rapidly decreasing depth can suddenly cause a huge and almost vertical wave to rear up from nowhere and break with sufficient violence to overwhelm almost any boat.

If such waves as these meet others running in a different direction, the results are similar to but far worse than that described for the interaction of differing wave-trains in a normal sea; particularly if the directions are wildly different as they will be when strong streams sweep out of bays to meet the main stream off a headland. The steep, confused and breaking seas that will be experienced in such places will be worsened considerably if a strong wind blows against the main stream, which will be accelerated as it gets squeezed past the headland (fig. 149). Such conditions cause the dangerous *races* found in places like the Pentland Firth off the north coast of Scotland and Portland Bill in the English Channel.

Similarly confused and unpredictable seas can be caused when waves run up against steep cliffs and harbour walls, and other such obstructions that lack a shallow approach to rob the waves of their energy. The waves can then be reflected and refracted so as to run back against or across the flow of their approaching brethren (fig. 150). This effect can cause unexpectedly dangerous and confused

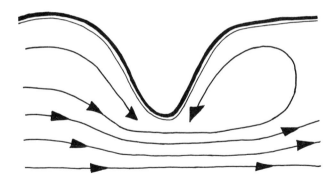

149 Headlands increase stream rate and may form eddies

150 The principal wavetrain comes in from seaward in the direction of the wide arrow (from bottom left). It reflects off the cliffs on the right of the bay and runs back across itself and also into the harbour. These reflected waves are also refracted around the harbour wall to run onto the beach to the left. The main wavetrain also reflects off and bends around the harbour wall, and the result is an extremely rough and confused sea all around the approaches and entrance to the harbour.

seas when approaching an apparently easily-entered harbour in strong onshore winds, and it can also occur when the wake of a large ship runs against the prevailing seas. Dangerous seas due to refraction also occur in the lee of some islands and shoals, in strong winds: waves 'bend' round each side and meet at an angle in the lee. In areas with a multitude of oil rigs close together, such as parts of the North Sea, there could be a very complex pattern of wave-trains causing generally disturbed and unpredictable sea conditions. The likelihood of encountering a wave much larger and steeper than the average, or an exceptionally deep trough, is clearly greater than normal where reflected or refracted waves occur.

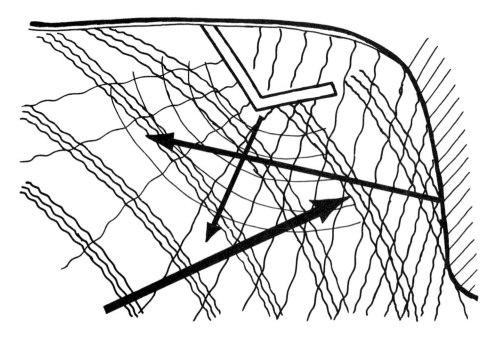

Handling a Boat in Rough Weather

In small seas you can simply accept the boat's various motions and proceed along your way in varying degrees of minor discomfort, depending on the shape of your hull. As the seas get bigger, however, so these effects will gradually produce greater and greater discomfort, and eventually danger. The less suitable your boat is for the conditions, the smaller the seas that will cause major discomfort and danger; the shape of a canal barge clearly bringing such things on far sooner than will that of a fishing vessel or lifeboat.

It should be apparent when discomfort reaches an unacceptable level, and steps can then be taken to improve things. Danger, however, is rather more insidious, as it is not always accompanied by discomfort, nor preceded by it. It can, nevertheless, be foreseen, and it can be felt.

Rolling

Dangerous rolling generally is preceded by discomfort, or at least alarm. It is an accepted fact that a roll of 20° feels like 45°, and one of 45° like a complete 90° knockdown. The chances of being literally rolled over by anything other than an exceptional wave are fairly small, unless synchronous rolling sets in. This will be quite unmistakeable as the rolling will suddenly become very regular and increasingly heavy. You should immediately change drastically the period of encounter of the waves by altering course or speed substantially; unless motoring beam-on when you must change course to do the first, as a change in speed will not affect the period of waves approaching from abeam. As a rule, it will be found better to alter course towards the waves for a safer and more comfortable ride, or to reduce speed rather than increase it. A steadying sail reduces the motion, and also the risk of synchronous rolling as it breaks the rhythm of the boat's roll.

In irregular seas there is an increased chance of being rolled right down by a big, steep one, and in rough weather races and other such areas should be avoided. At all times watch must be kept for an extra big wave, and the boat brought round to ride it on the bow rather than the beam, so as to reduce the risk of a dangerous roll.

Pitching

Bad pitching will damage a crew long before it does a well-found boat, and is the least dangerous of motions in rough weather. Violent, synchronous pitching can be remedied in the same way as synchronous rolling, by altering the period of encounter of the waves with a change of speed or course. A boat with fine entry and good flare will often ride better at increased speed, but course should be altered in a bluff-bowed vessel or pounding will get worse (figs 144 and 145). Bringing the sea slightly on the bow will improve her motion greatly, although the windage of a high bow could make steering more difficult. If you have the choice, alter so that your propeller effects help to turn her towards the wind, or set a mizzen. If she still pounds or pitches badly, slow down. In disturbed seas watch should be kept for the possibility of a very deep trough, so that the boat can be immediately slowed to reduce the impact as she falls into it.

Planing boats with a reasonably deep Vee hull should keep up speed so as to jump from wave to wave. Shallow Vee hulls, however, are like to pound very badly in such conditions and should be in harbour. Failing that, they should settle into a displacement mode and be handled as described above. When a displacement boat pitches badly or a planing boat jumps from wave to wave, there will be times when the propeller comes out of the water, where-upon with nothing solid to grip it will race furiously. A hand must be kept on the throttle at all times in such conditions so as to chop the power instantly the moment the prop races, and apply it again as it regains the water. Practice will enable you to anticipate the best moments and keep the boat going steadily.

Yawing

As the sea builds up, a boat will become increasingly difficult to steer downwind, and ever more prone to being sheered right round beam-on to the waves. This occurrence is called *broaching* and should be avoided at all costs, as in such a position a boat can easily be rolled right over by the following wave. If the waves are on the point of break-ing, the interference to their steady progression caused by the boat broaching could trigger off a following wave to break right over her. If this does not sink her immediately, her stability could be so reduced as to allow the next wave to capsize her. A vessel having a wave break over her stern is said to be *pooped*.

Running in a heavy sea requires intense concentration, as steering corrections to keep her straight must be made the instant the sea is felt under her stern, before the for-ward-moving water at the crest has a chance to carry it forward. The moment this happens, the water around the rudder will be moving forward with the boat and the rudder will not have any effect. You must then give her a blast of slipstream in order to provide steerage. For this reason you should never run at full throttle in such conditions, or you will have no reserve power. Anticipation of the steering correction may be quite difficult if the sea is directly astern, as you may not be certain which way the wave will take her until it is too late. Altering course slightly to bring the sea onto one quarter will resolve this problem, but it should be very slight as a sea on the quarter is more likely to broach you than one directly astern, having a head start on the swing.

If steering becomes sufficiently difficult that there appears to be a risk of broaching, you must slow down in order to allow the waves to pass under you more quickly. The closer your speed is to that of the waves, the longer your stern will sit in that forward-moving water at the crest, and the less will be the likelihood of you being able to maintain sufficient steering control to prevent her broaching. Slowing down may reduce steering control further, though, and the points made about using slipstream will become even more important.

A steadying sail for'ard may help to reduce yawing, but if the seas are big enough to blanket it from the wind when the boat is in a trough, the violent and sudden changes of pressure on it may actually make steering more difficult rather than less.

Deep-Vee planing boats can avoid this by travelling faster than the waves, leaping from crest to crest if they are close enough together. Throttles will have to be manipulated as described for pitching. If the waves are so long, however, that you can barely reach the next crest, there will be a serious risk of diving straight into the back of a wave and disappearing. You must then put the boat down into displacement mode and handle her as described above. This is likely to be difficult with the small rudders that such craft have, together with the poor directional stability of such a hull when immersed, and slipstream will have to be used to keep her steering. Great care must be taken to keep forward acceleration to a minimum during these bursts of power, or you could suddenly find yourself travelling at the same speed as the wave. Boats that steer with swivelling propellers will find all this even more difficult, and such boats may have to make early recourse to one of the severe weather tactics discussed in the next section.

Severe Conditions

In really big seas there may come a time, particularly with a boat that is small or less than ideal in shape, when you can no longer proceed with safety. This moment may come in relatively small seas if they are steep or irregular. The action to take can conveniently be split, depending on whether you are travelling upwind or downwind.

Upwind

Whether you are motoring beam-on to the seas or into them, there will come a time when the boat's motion forces you to go fairly slowly with the seas on one bow. The worse the weather gets the more slowly you will be forced to go on this heading, until finally you will be just stemming the seas and going nowhere. In power craft this position is referred to as *hove-to*, and is a recognised way of riding out severe weather.

The combination of water movement on the crests of the waves and windage on your bow will make it very difficult to hold the boat's head up to the wind in such bad conditions. This can be alleviated by heaving-to in such a direction that propeller effects assist your efforts to turn into the wind. A right-handed screw vessel, for example, should heave-to with the wind and sea on the port bow, and a twin-screw boat should run only her prop on the side opposite the wind. If a small mizzen can be rigged it will help greatly. The finer the lines of the boat, the more closely it will be possible to hold her bow into the waves while maintaining reasonable comfort.

Downwind

There will come a time with a following sea when it will be extremely difficult to keep from broaching, however slowly you motor. Boats with a lot of windage will be sailing by then, and if that windage is aft it will drive her too fast and also exacerbate the tendency to turn into the wind. It will not be possible to maintain any steering control with slipstream because of the risk of going too fast. You must then slow her down somehow, and also try to hold the stern into the wind.

Both aims can be achieved by towing big long warps in a bight from the stern (fig. 151). You should use the biggest and hairiest warps you can find, to provide the maximum drag, weighting the bight down with a tyre or coil of rope if necessary to keep it in the water and increase drag yet more. They should be as long as possible to prevent their disturbance in the water from causing a wave to break close astern. The drag enables slipstream to be used for steering, without risk of excessive speed.

This should only be resorted to if you are certain that you have plenty of sea room in which to continue running downwind until the weather relents, or that you can run gradually into sheltered water without having to alter course appreciably. If there is any chance that you will have to turn and heave-to in order to keep off a lee shore, then you should do so long before the seas get bad enough to warrant trailing warps, as turning round in a big sea can be

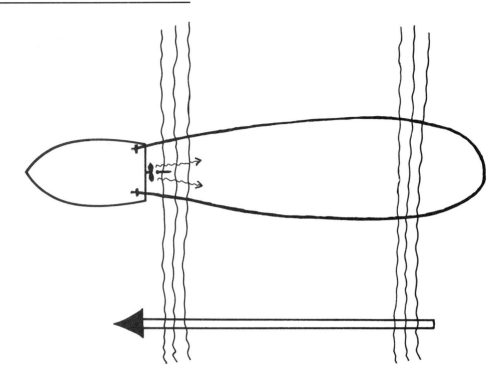

151 **Towing warps downwind**

a dangerous manoeuvre. The risk of being capsized or overwhelmed by a steep or breaking sea will be high during the time you are beam-on.

If you do have to turn in a big sea, remember the old adage about every seventh wave being the biggest. This may not be strictly or numerically the case, but it is a fact that waves are not regular in size, and very big ones are frequently followed by a brief spell of almost calm water as the overlying wave trains cancel each other out. You must watch the waves carefully for some while so as to try and predict when these calm patches occur, then time your turn so that you are beam-on to the seas just as a 'smooth' arrives. The turn must be started *before* the calm patch arrives (the moment the last wavecrest has passed under you), to ensure that its arrival coincides with your being beam-on to the sea, and it should be made under full power with the assistance of propeller effects in order to get round as quickly as possible. You can then heave-to with the prop assisting you to hold up into the wind, without having to go right round and put the waves on the other bow.

Crossing bars

This is rather a specialised case that involves traversing a short but dangerous stretch of water with calm seas and shelter beyond. The seas on the approach to the bar may be insufficient to warrant any special technique, but the dangers of crossing bars in strong onshore weather are such that it should never be attempted on the ebb (especially at springs) if at all possible. With a weak flood stream and plenty of depth (half-tide or more) conditions will be immeasurably safer.

If you have to cross at any other time, try to stand off and wait for a calm patch, as described above. Although it will be very difficult to gauge the state of the waves on the bar looking from seaward, if you can shoot over at the fastest safe speed you can muster, just before the arrival of a smooth patch so that it crosses the bar at the same moment, you will stand a fair chance of getting over safely. If you cannot be certain of doing this, trailing warps astern will help to reduce the danger of broaching, although pooping will always remain a risk. Batten down all hatches and secure all bodies in a cockpit with lifelines.

The Behaviour of Hull Types

From what has been discussed it should not be difficult to formulate the best sort of hull for riding out severe weather, and it can be seen on the ship's lifeboat in fig. 152. A long, straight keel with maximum depth aft, for good directional

152 Converted lifeboat

stability; a large, deep rudder and big, powerful prop for good steering control downwind and power upwind; a cruiser type stern to reduce yawing; a nicely-shaped bow, fine enough to cleave head seas but with sufficient buoyancy to avoid burying in troughs, and high enough to keep water off the deck but not enough to create excessive windage for'ard. Also, large bilge keels to reduce rolling; harmonious balance between height of topsides (to keep dry without too much overall windage) and depth of keel (for stability combined with a tolerable period of roll); the whole package held together with great plates of rivetted steel.

RNLI lifeboats are very similar in concept to this, but other boats are a compromise, depending on their purpose. Their behaviour and handling qualities at sea can be gauged roughly from how much, and in what way, they digress from this form of hull. A variety of commonly found hull types can be seen in fig. 9, shallow Vee; fig. 32, medium Vee; fig. 27, auxiliary sailing yachts; figs 28 and 136, displacement motor cruisers; fig. 153, fast semi-planing hull; and many other photos show various specific aspects of hull design.

153 **This type of hull, also known as *transitional*, is a compromise between a sea-going deep-Vee planing hull and a round-bilge displacement hull. It attempts to combine the performance of the former with the seakeeping qualities of the latter, and is much in use for fast workboats such as the one shown. A fine, flared bow leads to a round-bilge hull with flatter bottom and harder chines than a displacement boat, and then back to a wide transom with flat planing underbody. This shape causes her to lift partly out of the water, like a planing boat, for more speed; but retains the basic depth, shape and stability of a displacement boat**

10 Special Handling Techniques

There are certain manoeuvres that may have to be carried out under power in emergencies—when you are in trouble, or wish to help another boat. Although clearly much of the information so far discussed is likely to be called upon, there are some other techniques that you should find useful.

Grounding

The vulnerability to damage of protruding outboards, out-drives and twin screws is such that it is generally inadvisable to attempt motoring clear. An exception may be made if they are kept well clear of the bottom by a deep keel, such as on a motor-sailer, or if only the bow has gone on a steeply shelving bank. If damage is possible, you must kedge off. A single centreline screw, on the other hand, is generally sufficiently well protected by the keel for it to be safe to attempt motoring clear. However, remember that due to propeller slip the power that can be exerted with the engine is considerably less than can be applied by hauling out on an anchor.

If going full astern does not begin pulling her off almost immediately, the engine must be stopped: the wash of the prop turning astern will drive mud or sand forward and pile it under the hull, thus making it even more difficult to get her off. If the boat is small enough the grip of the bottom can often be loosened by rocking hard from side to side while going astern. The rolling action of the keel may widen the groove in which it is jammed. A deep-keel sailing boat can be heeled over to reduce her draft, although it should be apparent from fig. 154 that neither method will work with twin keels.

Another way is to put her slow ahead and wind the rudder fully back and forth a few times. This will pivot the keel around the grounding point and may widen the slot that is gripping it, particularly if the boat is aground for'ard. Then go astern.

Flat-bottomed boats can sometimes get stuck on a soft bottom, the suction preventing them from rising with the tide. This can be broken by stringing a chain under the hull

from side to side, then dragging and rattling it about to get some air or water between boat and mud, so breaking the suction. It is said that a sailing boat can be unstuck by walloping the top of the mast with a heavy hammer, so sending vibrations down through the hull.

154 **Twin keels can get stuck hard, or even get jammed on an obstruction between them**

Towing

There are three basic towing situations each requiring its own special technique: a short tow clear of an obstruction; towing in restricted waters; and towing at sea.

A short tow

This may be hauling someone off the mud, or perhaps plucking a sailing boat through a narrow gap or clear of a busy channel. If the disabled boat is afloat, with clear water all around her, you should approach close to her bow,

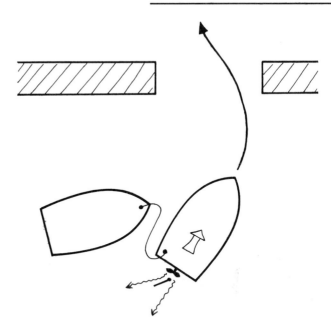

155 Taking up the tow

heading slowly in the direction in which you intend proceeding. The latter is important as you will find it difficult
to turn with the pull of the tow-rope on your stern. If,
however, this necessitates crossing her bow at a large
angle, you must appreciate that this pull will haul your
stern towards her as you take up the tow, especially if she
is heavy. Usually some compromise has to be made, as you
can see in fig. 155.

Steering and control will be much improved if you can
secure the tow-rope amidships, or even for'ard. You can
then turn your boat around the point of the tow (fig. 156).

**156 Towing from a
forward point**

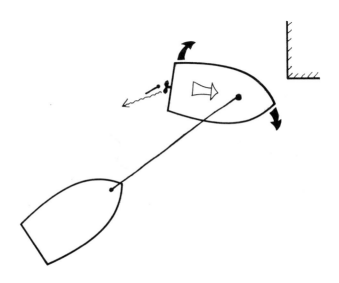

Note the towing bollard on the marina launch in fig. 157. If there is any risk of the tow taking charge, say in strong winds, you must be careful not to let the tow-rope lead out to the side or there will be a risk of *girding* or *girting* (the tow pulling hard enough to capsize you). The tow-rope must always be secured so that it can be cast off quickly and easily while under strain. Care must also be taken to keep it clear of your prop if it slackens.

With the tow-rope passed, and secured at a suitable length (just long enough that the tow will not run into you when you slow down) go very slow ahead and take up the strain as gradually as possible, if necessary using brief touches ahead until the tow-rope is taut. Then keep your speed steady in order to keep it taut; the towed boat should steer to the outside of turns in order to do the same. Any slackening of the rope followed by sudden tightening can create considerable snatching strains on the gear.

157 Forward towing post on a marina launch

If a strong wind is blowing, before you pass the tow-rope it is important to consider any major differences in drift characteristics there may be between the two boats, if you are to avoid them blowing together (see chapter 3). In a strong wind it is generally best to come up to her bow from leeward, passing far enough ahead to avoid it blowing down on you as the tow-rope is passed.

If you are pulling a boat off the mud you will need to consider the stream as well, although a strong wind is likely to be the major problem. You will be very limited as to the angle of approach you can take, and there could be serious risk, if he has blown onto the mud, of the same thing happening to you. Very often the best way to deal with this situation is to approach directly downwind, using the draw of the wind on the stern to hold you clear of the shallow water as the tow-rope is passed, and also to ensure that you come straight out astern with the casualty in tow from your bow. If you attempt to tow him from your stern and come out ahead, the wind is likely to blow your bow in very rapidly as you try to turn up into it with the tow-rope restricting the swing of your stern.

If you doubt your boat's capacity to haul the casualty straight off astern into the wind, you must approach along the line of the bank and pass him a long enough tow-rope to enable you to power round into the wind and get well upwind before taking up the tow. This will give you room to play with. It may be better, however, to anchor upwind and drop down as close to him as you can. You can then haul him off with the windlass, or at least use the cable to keep your head upwind as you take the strain. Sailing boats can, if firmly aground, be hauled off with a tow-rope to the masthead, so reducing their draft considerably as the pull heels them over. There is a risk of damage, however.

Towing in restricted waters

If you have to do any tight manoeuvring with a casualty in tow, you will find control extremely difficult if he is hanging off your stern. Crossing a pair of short tow-ropes to each of your quarters will make him follow you more closely without sheering (fig. 158), but the restriction of your steering limits the method to towing boats very much smaller than your own. The best control will be obtained by towing him alongside: both boats can then be towed together as one, with certain limitations.

In fig. 159 you can see two boats secured together for an alongside tow. The warps are exactly as for securing alongside a quay, but the tug should be positioned some-what abaft the towed boat's stern, so that the latter's hull does not interfere with the flow of water round rudder and propeller. All warps should be as taut as possible so that

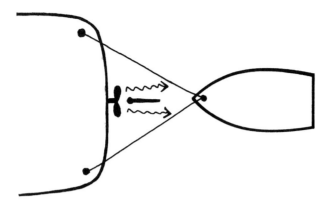

158 **Double tow lines**

the boats cannot swing about separately, and they must be well fendered all along.

You can then proceed as one vessel, though bearing in mind that the handling of your boat will be greatly affected by the one alongside. Her dead weight in the water will reduce acceleration and stopping power, and also tend to pull your bow round towards her, causing you to turn much more readily in that direction than away from her. If you can plan ahead the turning you are likely to have to do, you should secure her on the side towards which you intend making the sharpest turns. Otherwise position her so that your propeller effects will assist a turn away from her: i.e. on your starboard side if you have a right-handed prop. This will also help to keep you straight when going astern.

The final manoeuvring into a berth may require some ingenuity, and even repositioning the tow further ahead of your bow or on the other side. You may be able to cast him off, then nudge him into position with your bow against a good fender, but be careful not to let yourself get into an awkward position. In strong winds or streams warps and checklines may have to be got ashore. In fig. 160 you can see one way of pushing the tow into his berth. The tug will be quite manoeuvrable in this position: able to push steadily ahead as shown, to spring the tow round the corner; or go

159 **Towing alongside**

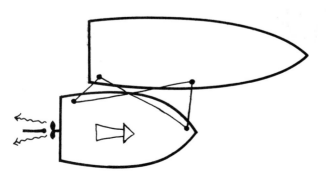

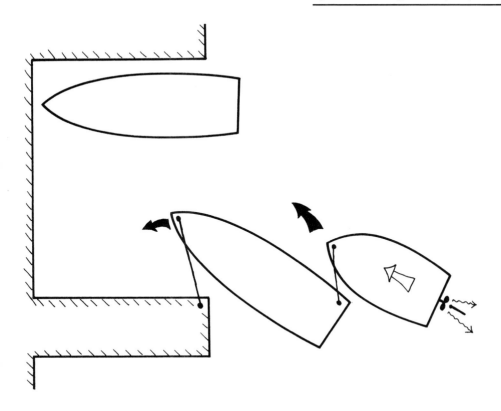

160 Nudging the tow into a berth

astern to change the forespring onto the tow into a head rope and then use it to stop her; or turn athwart the tow and push on her quarter to get her stern across.

Towing at sea

Because of the presence of waves, and the consequent considerable movement of the two boats in relation to each other, it is quite impractical to tow by either of the previous two methods. The casualty must be towed astern, and provision has to be made for the constant slackening and tightening that will occur in the tow-rope. In anything of a seaway this will be more than enough to part any tow-rope, or rip cleats and bollards out of the deck.

There are three ways of providing the necessary give in the tow-rope: using nylon warp, with its great capacity for stretching then instantly returning to normal; inserting a large motor tyre roughly midway along the tow-rope, which will weight it down and have a similar, though lesser, effect; and hanging a heavy weight in the middle of the tow-rope so that it hangs down in the water in an arc, shock loads being absorbed in lifting the weight and straightening the arc as they are when anchored to heavy cable. This is usually most easily done by simply securing the tow-rope

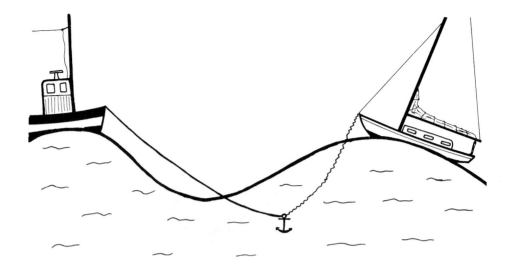

to the towed boat's anchor shackle, and getting him to veer sufficient length of cable that the tow-rope always lies below the water (fig. 161). The tow-rope should never be allowed to spring up out of the water.

Your approach should generally be made from leeward, passing the tow-rope as you cross his bow, and the length adjusted if possible so that both boats rise to the crests of waves simultaneously; this will help to reduce shock loads. The tow should lead from the very stem of the towed boat, (though not necessarily be made fast there); this enables her to steer straight with minimal risk of sheering. Both ends of the tow must be made fast to very strong points—the base of a mast, right round a deckhouse, right round the deck and secured to all major cleats and the windlass—and be well protected from chafe where they pass through fairleads. It is good policy to adjust the length of the tow slightly from time to time so a different part of the warp is brought into the fairlead and subjected to chafe. This is known as *freshening the nip*.

The speed of the tow should not exceed the designed maximum speed of the towed boat or her bow-wave will move right aft, causing her stern to lift up on it and her bow to dip into the preceding trough. This will make her yaw badly and she may even start to break up or be towed right under (as has happened to yachts towed by ships, which could not go slowly enough). Small displacement vessels may have designed speeds of as little as 5 knots (calculated roughly by multiplying the square root of the waterline length in feet by 1.4, for an average boat). Narrow boats will have a slightly faster maximum speed than given by this formula, and beamy boats a slower one.

Dangerous yawing can also occur if the towed boat has poor directional stability. Modern short-keeled yachts can

161 **Keeping a catenary in the tow line**

be a problem in this respect, and are unlikely to tow well without being competently steered. Any boat that is deeper for'ard than aft (such as many planing boats) will yaw very badly, due to the lack of grip in the water aft. It is generally best to tow such craft stern first if weather permits, when they will follow your wake far more accurately. This technique should also be used for a tow of any length in narrow waters. Yawing from poor directional stability may be improved by towing warps to provide a drag on the stern.

Dinghies and any really small light craft can be a real problem to tow at sea, especially in following waves when they will roam about all over the place, attempt to overtake you, and possibly even try to come aboard via a passing wave! They should be secured with two painters, one to each quarter of the towing boat, in order to reduce yawing (see fig. 158). It may be effective to stream warps behind the towed boat, as described above, to slow it down and stop surging. Long painters may also keep them clear of the parent vessel.

Dinghies should be trimmed down by the stern, and the tow-ropes are best taken from low down on the stem, so reducing the draft for'ard and increasing it aft at the skeg (fig. 162). A sailing dinghy with no skeg aft is usually best towed stern first, as for a planing boat (which is what it is).

162 A low towing eye and short painter lifts the bow

Inflatables are a law unto themselves, having neither weight nor directional stability. In a following wind they are quite likely to blow right up onto the afterdeck, where they should be promptly lashed down and left!

Man Overboard

There are two distinct facets to this problem: returning to the person in the water, and actually getting him back on board. The second also applies to fishing anybody out of the water.

Finding the person

Reaction to someone's going overboard should be immediate, quite instinctive, and as follows:

1 Yell 'Man overboard starboard (or port)'
2 Throw lifebelt over the appropriate side
3 Watch the person constantly
4 Put helm hard over to swing stern away from him
5 Press Decca 'man overboard marker' if fitted

Only when these actions have been taken should you pause to think about your next move, which will depend on the prevailing situation. The order in which these initial actions should be carried out is not necessarily as shown. They should all be done as near together as is humanly possible, and at least one person in the crew should be detailed immediately to watch the man constantly—regardless of anything else that might be happening. It should be stressed to him that it is vital not to take his eyes off the casualty for so much as a split second: kept constantly in view, someone in the water can be seen for surprisingly long distances, far greater than it would be possible to sight him again having lost him.

If sea and visibility are good enough for the man to be held in view during a complete 180° turn of the boat, you should simply keep going hard round, whereupon she will return more or less to the spot where the helm was put hard over. Slow down as you approach someone, and pick him up as described in the next section. Do not, under any circumstances, allow the man to get out of sight, however, even though it may be obvious that you are heading towards him.

If sea and visibility conditions are not good enough to be sure of keeping him in sight, you should, after initially turning the stern away from the man, execute what is known as a *Williamson Turn* (fig. 163). Meanwhile the watchers keep concentrating on the casualty. The initial

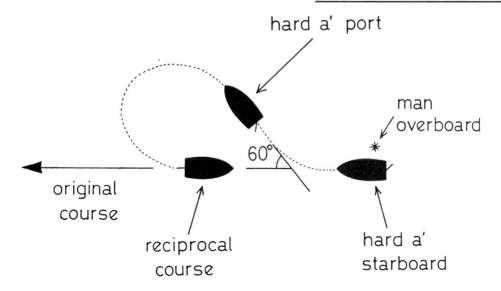

hard a' port

man overboard

60°

original course

reciprocal course

hard a' starboard

163 Williamson Turn

turn should be continued until the boat is heading about 60° from her previous course, then full opposite helm should be applied to turn her the other way. The opposite turn is continued until she can be steadied on the reciprocal of her original course, normal speed being maintained throughout the complete evolution. The boat will now be more or less on the line of her original course, and the casualty should be sighted somewhere ahead.

If you are sharp enough to note the time taken between the first alteration of course (as the man went over) and the final steadying on the reciprocal course, you should then maintain normal speed on this course for a further period equal to half this time, in order to return to the spot where course was first altered. The casualty should then be very close ahead of you. Be very careful, however, not to run over him. If you have a Decca Navigator with a man overboard marker, you can return to the position marked. This should, however, be used in conjunction with all the aforementioned techniques, and not in place of them. It most certainly should not substitute for the immediate steps, especially keeping a constant watch on the man; nor should hunting for the requisite button be allowed to distract anyone from the basic manoeuvre.

You should assiduously practice both these techniques, so that you know just where to expect to be on completion of either turn, and also to assess the precise offset angle that returns your boat to the reciprocal course in the Williamson Turn. The stated 60° is an approximation only, as is the timing. If you turn inside your original wake, then this angle is too great.

Recovery

There is considerable debate as to the best way of getting someone back aboard, and it will anyway depend very much on sea conditions, the design of the boat, the number of crew you have available, and the person's condition.

Two very real dangers must be considered when approaching a person in the water: the risk of catching him in turning propellers, and the possibility of the boat riding over him—due to approaching too fast, wind blowing the boat over the top of him, or a wave picking her up and dropping her on him when he is alongside.

In reasonable conditions the best way to avoid all these risks is to come up slightly to weather (far enough to be certain you will not run him down), and stop the boat with the person about amidships. The engine itself should also be stopped, to avoid any chance of him being drawn into

164 A bathing platform helps getting down close to a casualty

a creeping conventional prop or revolving variable pitch one, or the gear lever being accidentally knocked. Then the boat is allowed to drift down to him, and the first priority is to get a line to, and around, him. A conscious man can usually be got aboard with little trouble using a boarding ladder that extends a few feet below the surface, and a line with a bowline under his armpits for support and the reassurance of a safe connection to the yacht.

If the casualty is cold or helpless, you may have to send someone into the water to put the bowline round him, while wearing a lifejacket and safety line. If the boat is rolling it may be relatively easy to heave someone aboard as the boat rolls down. The liferaft boarding technique of bouncing the victim up and down in the water a couple of times to build up momentum, then heaving him aboard as his buoyancy shoots him upwards, is a useful (if disconcerting) trick if you have a low platform aft to get him onto (fig. 164), but get a good grip on him first.

If the weather is rough, however, there could be considerable risk of the boat blowing, or being thrown, on top of the casualty unless he can be hauled aboard very quickly. It may be better to approach him heading almost directly into the wind and waves, keeping them slightly on one bow so as to create something of a lee on the other side for the pickup. You can then keep your drift to a minimum, while at the same time ensuring that you move towards him and do not blow away. He should be picked up amidships where the freeboard and motion are least, and there is no risk of the stem or stern lifting and dropping onto him.

Rescue Work

Much of this has already been covered in the preceding sections, but some particular care has to be taken when rescuing people who are in the water with capsized craft, such as boardsailors and dinghy sailors. (For details of how to extricate the people from the water see above.) A surf or sailing board can then be hauled aboard with little ceremony, other than ensuring that no sails or even short lines get near your prop. Rescuing a capsized dinghy, however, is a rather more complicated affair.

Righting sailing dinghies

If the boat is lying on her side in the water, her sails and rigging will normally act like a sea anchor and the hull will drift round them until the mast is pointing upwind. The best approach is then to come downwind towards the top of the mast, as this enables you to use the draw of the wind to keep your prop well clear of sails, rigging and the many ropes that will be trailing around in the water. A hand right for'ard can then either lean over the bow or reach down with a boathook, grab the top of the mast and pull it up out of the water.

As the sail comes out of the water the wind catching it will tend to swing the bow of the dinghy into the wind, and your foredeck crew should make use of this by handing down the forestay, so that as the boat comes further up out of the water she is allowed to swing round his grip on the forestay until she is finally upright and lying head-to-wind at your bow. During all this you must keep your stern upwind by judicious use of the propeller, but at the same time follow instructions from the foredeck crew as he may need you to move the bow around and forward as he hauls up on the forestay, particularly if the dinghy is heavy and very dead in the water.

Still remaining stern to the wind, as the dinghy will readily capsize again if she does not remain head to it, you can haul her alongside your boat and put someone aboard to get the sails down and bail out the water. The latter may entail stuffing something into the top of the centreboard case to prevent the water pouring in faster than it can be got out. She can then be towed to safety as described earlier. If there are large drain flaps at the stern you can, in calm water, tow her full of water with the bow hauled up high at your stern, in order to drain her. Speed should be very slow to begin with or the weight of water could pull out her transom.

If a dinghy is completely upside down, slide a boathook down her forestay as far as possible and pull her up until the mast is level with the water. You will have to be careful to hold your boat clear of where the mast and sails will appear. Do this so that the mast comes up to weather of the dinghy, then you can proceed as described above. If the mast is to leeward, you will find it harder to pull upright against the wind, more difficult to maintain your attitude while stopped head-to-wind, and with a greater likelihood of your boat becoming tangled up with the dinghy. In rough weather it is generally better to stand off until the mast swings upwind.

Having said all this, most competent dinghy sailors can quite easily right their craft, and should always be encouraged to do so if they can, as this will involve considerably less trouble and risk than if you do it. Stand off well clear and shout encouragement until you are certain they are safely under way again, and intervene only if they appear quite incapable or exhausted. Much unpleasantness, and danger, can be caused by powerboat skippers interfering in such an operation when they are not needed. Fig. 165

should give you an idea of the mass of tangled sails and rigging that will be floating around a capsized dinghy; the centreboard case is at the for'ard end of the cockpit under the boom and sail.

Taking crew off a boat

It is difficult to give simple advice as to how best to do this, as circumstances vary so much. In general, approach should be made from leeward so as to pass close to the casualty's bow, as for passing a towline. People should be told to jump when the relative movement between the two boats is least, usually when the smaller one is on top of a wave, neither falling nor rising. Stand by to firmly grab each one as he lands. A delicate but very firm touch will be required on throttle and steering, although the power of slipstream should be remembered if the bow needs rapidly turning, particularly into the wind. It is not wise to hang about under the lee bow of a large drifting vessel and a number of fairly quick passes is generally advisable, taking crew off one or two at a time if necessary.

165 **Capsized, most dinghies dump a tangle of lines into the water**

11 Breakdowns and Bad Weather

Although not strictly a part of handling boats under power, mechanical problems affect your ability to do so. Let us consider those likely to be encountered, and see how a boat can continue to be handled.

Engine failure

If a standby engine is available, such as a second twin, a wing engine or an outboard, you can often continue on this until the broken unit is repaired. To be fully effective, however, the standby should be completely independent of the main engine—twin engines, for example, should have totally separate fuel tanks and systems—so that no kind of fault can affect them both.

At the same time, however, dual fuel tanks linked with stop valves let both engines run off either tank, or one engine can take fuel from both tanks. This will give you considerable flexibility to cope with engine breakdowns, fuel contamination and fuel feed problems. Remember, however, the comments made in Chapter 8 about stability if running off one tank only.

It is important to appreciate the handling problems that are likely when running on a low-powered offset wing engine, an outboard, or one engine of a pair of twins. If an outboard can be fixed in the middle of the stern and swivelled for steering there will be no problem other than lack of power. If headway cannot be maintained, it may be necessary to make for a different harbour or patiently await a change in tidal stream. Carefully check the fuel situation, and anchor if possible to conserve fuel until the tide turns fair. You may find it very difficult to keep her head up into the wind when motoring or heaving-to; all effort should be made to rig some sort of mizzen.

These comments apply equally to motoring with a low-powered wing engine, and the difficulties may be either worsened or lessened by propeller effects, depending on their direction. One engine of twins will probably provide sufficient power for most, if not all, conditions; but propeller effects are likely to be even greater than with the wing engine, as the prop will almost certainly be bigger and further from the centreline.

Consider manoeuvring in terms of a single offset prop a long way from the centreline, although the single twin may have its own rudder behind it giving good slipstream when turning either way. With an outward-turning prop the boat will turn most readily away from the prop—so readily that keeping a straight course may be difficult if there is a strong wind blowing the bow in the same direction. Course may have to be adjusted to bring the wind to a less damaging angle (abeam perhaps), and a zig-zag route followed in order to get home.

Turning into the wind may have to be accomplished by first going astern into it (the draw of the wind overcoming the adverse prop effects), then turning the other way so as to place the prop on the outside of the turn. With the prop in this position you should be able to hold her up to the wind without trouble (fig. 166). A similar technique may be found necessary with a wing engine. Heaving-to would have to be done with the wind on the side opposite the prop.

Manoeuvring in harbour and into a berth are likely to pose similar problems, together with the difficulty of actually coming alongside neatly. If conditions of wind and stream are far from helpful, you may have to settle for

166 Turning into the wind

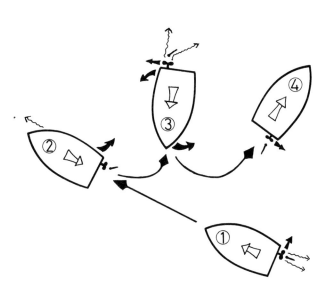

getting some part of the boat into the berth, then pass warps ashore and work her in with them (see Chapter 6). Think carefully about how your working prop will behave in the prevailing conditions.

With just the inside prop you should berth as though extreme prop effects were hindering the swing in on going astern. It will probably be best to approach steeply and stop just before the berth, then kick her round and alongside before going astern to stop. When berthing on an outside prop the normal approach should be made, using prop effects astern to swing her alongside. If you have trouble getting her square into the berth, try going astern on a forward backspring, as in fig. 167, or ahead on a turning forespring.

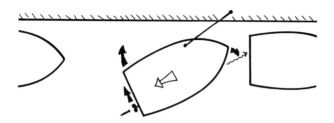

167 **Berthing on the outside prop**

Fouled propeller or rudder

It is all too easy to get a trailing rope round the prop when motoring, especially among moorings, and great care should be taken to keep ropes away from the stern. Lines from fishing floats out at sea are another hazard, especially at night. If the rudder is on a separate skeg then it is a good idea to fix a wire from the skeg to the keel, to make ropes slide clear underneath. It is also possible to fit to propshafts special rope cutters.

A rope round the rudder can often be pushed down and clear with a long pole with a rowlock lashed to the end, or possibly by lowering a length of chain onto it with a long line. If it jams between the hull and the top of the rudder, you will probably have to cut it and haul it clear from the other side. A rope round the prop or shaft is more of a problem. If the engine does not stop anyway, then stop it and ensure that it cannot fire up as you try to pull the rope off: remove the plug leads, or decompress the cylinders in a diesel. Then try to unwind it by hauling on one end of the rope while turning the propshaft by hand in the opposite direction to the way it was running when it fouled. Usually, however, no amount of pulling and turning will shift it. Artificial fibres tend to wrap round a shaft, then melt into a solid mass. The only solution is to cut it off with a hacksaw or serrated blade; smooth blades are quite ineffectual, however sharp. This generally entails hanging over the side of the dinghy with it lashed to a boathook or something, or going into the water.

Steering breakdown

If the steering fails on a twin-screw boat, you should be able to make a reasonable job of steering her by varying the speed of each engine as required. At any speed this will require a delicate touch, and I suggest you practise it. In manoeuvring, the control obtained from the opposing prop effects makes steering gear almost redundant anyway.

With a single screw, however, life is rather more difficult as the boat will simply go round and round in circles, whatever you do with the throttle. Unless you can rig a proper jury rudder you will need to provide some form of drag on the appropriate quarter in order to keep her straight. You should also experiment with engine speed and course to find the combination that produces the least turning effect.

There are a number of ways in which you can exert drag on the quarter opposite the side to which she turns, but whatever the method it must be easy to alter so that you can adjust the amount of drag to produce the steering effect required. A bight of heavy warp streamed from the quarter can be effective, and its drag can be controlled by the length, though altering it may take time. Tyres or such-like can be attached to the bight to increase the drag. A heavy dinghy secured alongside opposite the turn may also be found effective, especially if large buckets can be trailed over its stern. (Think back to the comments made in chapter 10 about towing alongside.) The further outboard the drag can be streamed the more effect it will have, and if you have a boom or derrick you could bring that into play to hold out the lines.

If you can rig sails, they may enable you to overcome prop effects, and steer the boat with some accuracy by adjusting their position and sheeting (see Chapter 8). For slow manoeuvring in restricted waters this might be more practical than towing a drag. If your destination happens to be upwind, you may be able to utilise the draw of the wind on your stern to make a fairly accurate, if slow, sternboard. Before doing any of these, however, try your emergency tiller: the steering fault may lie in the linkages rather than the rudder.

Serious Listing

The effect that this can have on steering was discussed in Chapter 2, and its effect on stability in chapter 8. All attempts should be made to correct a list by transferring weights, or pumping fuel or water to different tanks if possible. If liquids cannot be transferred, taking on extra weight by filling an empty tank with sea water may be preferable to proceeding with a heavy list, for reasons explained in Chapter 8. You may be able to do this at sea by rearranging the plumbing of a bilge pump, or by using a deckwash hose. Any major alteration in fore-and-aft trim should also be compensated for.

Survival Weather Tactics

The chances of encountering conditions too severe for the tactics described in Chapter 9 are extremely remote: so remote, in fact, that even the most experienced of writers on the subject of heavy weather admit to having only limited and circumstantial evidence as to the effectiveness of traditional survival techniques.

I have no experience at all of using in earnest any of these techniques, but I shall comment briefly on them as best I can, culling from others what seems to be a sensible and general consensus. Although you may never find your-self in true survival weather as such, an engine or steering breakdown in moderately bad weather could prevent you from handling the seas as described in Chapter 9, and the following comments may help you keep the boat in a safe position.

Lying a-hull

This consists simply of shutting down the engines, bat-tening down the hatches, and leaving the boat to her own devices. She will then drift with wind and sea, adopting an attitude consistent with her hull shape and windage, probably beam-on to the waves. Though sailing yachts have done this successfully, there seems to be little to recommend the technique for a power boat with her limited safe angle of heel: all efforts should be made to prevent her lying beam-on to the waves. Try to rig a small steadying sail to combat the risk of synchronous rolling, placed for'ard or aft to make her take up a safer angle to the waves.

Streaming a sea anchor

The traditional sea anchor is a large, heavy canvas cone

with a hole in each end, designed to be streamed from the bow to hold it into the waves when heaving-to with no, or insufficient power. As the boat drifts backwards the sea anchor holds back the bow sufficiently to ensure that it stays well upwind of the stern. Certainly drift is slowed significantly, but great strain is put on cleats, etc.

The consensus seems to be that unless the boat has negligible windage for'ard and a long, directionally stable keel, it simply does not work for power boats, being generally incapable of holding the bow closer than about 45° to the seas. It also pulls the bow down, preventing it lifting to the seas, and the rapid drift and jarring astern puts great stresses on the rudder. Some writers claim that it is better streamed from the stern, thus protecting the rudder and utilising the windage of the bow to keep the boat stern-on to the seas. There would seem to be some logic to this, especially for boats with high bows and cruiser sterns (as on the fishing vessel type) which would ride the seas more easily than wide transoms, and rise to them more readily than fine bows. However, the openings (windows, doors, hatches) on most craft are better able to withstand green water striking them from ahead than from aft.

In the absence of a sea anchor it seems to be worth trailing warps, etc in the hope of at least preventing her from lying beam-on and of slowing down her drift if sea room is limited. For power boats, with their high superstructures and lack of deep keels, drift can be very fast. A small mizzen or some sort of canvas aft should help her to lie further upwind: the old fishing drifters used to ride out gales while lying to their nets streamed from the bow and with a small mizzen set. In shallow water it may be worth streaming the anchor cable (without the anchor), in the hope that the drag on the bottom will hold her head upwind and reduce drift.

Dispersing oil

Very small quantities of heavy oil do have an almost magical ability to smooth out breaking seas and render them harmless. Ordinary engine oil appears to be perfectly suitable, and oil plus detergent has proved equally calming. The problem seems to be that the slick drifts more slowly than the boat, so getting it where you want it is somewhat easier than keeping it there. The traditional way of dispersing oil is through stuffed canvas bags with very small holes pricked in them, or by pumping it out through the heads. I suspect that it is probably most practical for calming localised areas of very rough water such as races and overfalls or possibly harbour bars before entering. Handling the oil in rough conditions, and especially keeping it from making the deck dangerously and instantly slippery, is not easy.

Appendix

Unusual Propulsion Systems

To avoid unnecessary complication, this book has dealt with only the propulsion and steering systems commonly in use on powerboats and auxiliary sailing craft. There are, however, some rare and specialised systems that you may come across, and a few of them are described here to enable you to handle them competently in the light of the contents of the rest of the book.

Contra-rotating propellers

Here two propellers are in effect on the same shaft—although actually driven separately, one shaft running inside the other—and turning in opposite directions. As the props are identical their opposing effects cancel out. Some big outdrive units have them, described as *Duoprops* and claimed to give increased acceleration and top speed. Handling will be as for a swivelling prop, but with no paddlewheel effect. Propeller effects in a twin-screw installation will be offset only.

Surface drive propeller

An inboard installation where the propeller runs with its boss more or less on the surface so that only its lower half is immersed. It enables very high speed craft to reduce drag greatly by raising shafting and brackets clear of the water.

A small rudder is directly abaft the prop for steering, and handling is essentially the same as that with a conventional fixed prop and rudder. When under way the prop actually draws water up and around itself completely, so that the upper half is not actually working in air: this produces a distinctive 'rooster tail' wake. An effect of the prop being only half submerged is that it trims the boat automatically without the need for trim-tabs.

A recent alternative to high-powered outdrives, surface piercing props are cheaper and better able to accept the considerable torque of powerful diesel engines through the inboard gearbox. They will be vulnerable to damage, stuck out of the transom on the surface.

Waterjets

These employ a small propeller inside a casing at the stern, driving the boat by thrusting a jet of water out through a nozzle. It is useful in very shallow or weed-ridden water where a conventional prop would be damaged or fouled, or when working around swimmers. Waterjets are steered by swivelling deflector plates at the end of the nozzle, and reversed by redirecting the jet forward with a semi-circular 'bucket'. Handling is more or less as with an outdrive unit, although there will be no paddlewheel effect at all.

Ahead-only propeller

An option on very small outboards and some small yacht auxiliaries. The latter generally provide ahead and neutral through the gearbox, while some outboards have no neutral at all, the prop turning ahead the moment the engine fires. Although slipstream can be used for turning, generally such a boat must be handled as though under sail, coasting in neutral to a gradual stop. You should aim to be stopped just short of your destination, so that a brief kick ahead with slipstream can push you into the right spot with some precision.

Propeller behind the rudder

You may come across the occasional auxiliary yacht with this arrangement, its total inefficiency when manoeuvring at slow speeds being the price paid for tucking it right up under the stern out of the way. There will be no slipstream effect at all, and the rudder will work only when the hull is moving through the water. The disadvantages of this arrangement should be obvious (fig. 168).

Inward-turning offset propeller

If the prop is close enough to the centreline for its slipstream to flow over the rudder, the paddlewheel effect of this configuration will combine with slipstream to turn the boat sharply towards the side with the prop. She will turn the other way very sluggishly: with paddlewheel effect hindering, slight offset effect helping, and no slipstream. You may have to gather speed, then stop the prop to eliminate paddlewheel effect, so that the flow of water past the rudder can turn her. Behaviour going astern will be unpredictable and variable, due to the offset effect being opposed by changing paddlewheel effect.

Offset variable pitch propeller

If you encounter one of these, you had better put on your thinking cap! If it is inward-turning it will behave as above when going ahead, but as an outward-turning offset prop when going astern. If it is outward-turning it will behave so in ahead, but as above in astern; all because the direction of rotation does not change from ahead to astern, as it does with a normal prop.

Inward-turning twin screws

Although they will balance each other out when running straight, behaviour at slow speeds will be unpredictable due to each prop having a strong offset effect opposed by a variable paddlewheel effect, particularly when going astern. Control ahead will be improved with twin rudders. With a single rudder, see the comments above on an inward-turning offset prop.

168 A prop behind the rudder

Unhanded twin screws

Twin screws that both rotate in the same direction negate all the manoeuvring advantages of outward-turning handed twins, though they are encountered. Handling will be much as with a single outward-turning offset prop, although slipstream will be usable when turning ahead either way, assuming twin rudders. The boat will thus turn far more readily in the direction that is assisted by paddlewheel effect; the boat in fig. 29, Chapter 2 has a pair of left-handed twin screws and will turn more readily to starboard. A three-point turn, however, should be made to port (as for a single screw) to utilise the strong prop effects of the port screw when going astern. Think carefully about how each prop will behave on its own.

Triple screws

Some old naval fast patrol boats may be found with triple screws, which was simply a way of getting a lot of power into the water through lightweight engines and small props. They also had triple rudders, one behind each prop, with the starboard and centre props right-handed and the port one left-handed. Thus they could be manoeuvred as normal twin-screw craft with outward turning props simply by shutting down the centre engine.

Quadruple screws

These are normally installed as a pair of right-handed props to starboard and a pair of left-handed to port. Maximum side-thrust when manoeuvring is gained by using only the two outside ones, when handling will be as for outward-turning twins although with greater sidethrust as the props are likely to be a long way from the centreline.

Kitchen rudder

An interesting device, sometimes called 'bucket steering', which was used on certain old naval launches. A fixed propeller is encased in two hemispherical 'buckets', port and starboard, which can be pivoted to divert the whole of the propeller slipstream.

They are also opened and closed in order to act as both throttle and gearlever, the propeller turning at a constant speed all the time. With the buckets fully open at their after end, full speed ahead is obtained; while progressively closing them slows down the boat by diverting some of the slipstream forward. With the buckets closed sufficiently to split the fore and aft slipstreams equally, neutral gear is

169 **This unusual rudder has clearly been made for improving slipstream effect when turning. When swivelled it should gather the slipstream from both sides of the prop, instead of just one side as a conventional rudder does**

effectively obtained. Further closing drives the boat increasingly fast astern. Handling is similar to a swivelling prop, but with no paddlewheel effect.

For'ard rudder

An old-fashioned and simpler version of the bow thruster, it still needs a flow of water across it before it will work: so, with no propeller for'ard the boat must be moving relative to the water (or vice versa) for it to have any effect. It is commonly employed by large Continental canal barges for manoeuvring in the restricted spaces of canals, and is particularly useful for getting round tight bends without drifting onto the outer bank since it pulls the bow round sharply without swinging the stern out.

A for'ard rudder can do more or less all the things that a

170 **Is this a sailing boat that exerts her drive through a propeller, or a motor boat whose engine is fuelled by wind? The huge air propeller is revolved by the wind, just like a windmill, and drives an underwater prop through shafts and gears. The small outdrive unit at the stern is an auxiliary. She is rumoured to be efficient, capable of sailing directly into the wind, and afflicted with negligible heeling force from the windmill. The complexities of her handling are, however, somewhat beyond the scope of this book; although I suspect a variable pitch water propeller would have much to recommend it, enabling the pitch to be adjusted to suit the variable power transmitted from the windmill**

171 **The behaviour of the for'ard rudder for tightening a turn or pushing a boat sideways should be clear from the diagrams; and its uses, particularly for counteracting wind on the bow, apparent. When the boat is motoring in a straight line, the effect of putting the for'ard rudder over is to push the bow across with no corresponding outward swing of the stern, as the water flow impinges on the side of the stern and tends to push it across the same way the bow is going. This is especially useful for rounding tight bends in a long vessel, and is so pronounced that the stern can actually swing in towards the inner bank, requiring a touch of outswing on the aft rudder to keep it off.**

bow thruster can do, more cheaply but not quite so well, and only when the boat is moving through the water. The relationship between the handling and effectiveness of the two is similar to that between a swivelling propeller and a rudder with no propeller slipstream (fig. 171). On rivers with a strong current, there may be enough flow over the rudder at low speed over the ground for it to be useful.

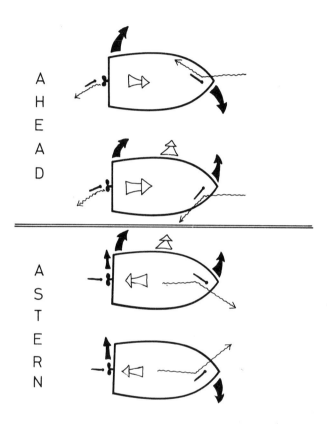

A
H
E
A
D

A
S
T
E
R
N

Kort Nozzle

A tube encasing the propeller and extending aft of it concentrates the slipstream directly astern, almost like a jet, and increases noticeably the power of a given prop at low speeds. It is often fitted to towing vessels such as trawlers and tugs. Slipstream effect will be increased, and paddlewheel effect reduced due to the nozzle preventing the prop from wheeling water out sideways. There is also protection against catching ropes and nets in the prop. They are reputed to reduce the likelihood of the prop racing when a boat pitches heavily in a head sea, the nozzle tending to contain water round the prop when the stern lifts clear of the sea or near the surface.

Propellers in Tunnels

These are often found on old lifeboats and river launches, and have the advantage of keeping the props protected from weed and damage. The higher prop also enables a more horizontal shaft to be installed, which increases efficiency as less effort is wasted trying to push the stern upwards. There is less likelihood of ventilation or cavitation as the props are kept in water away from the surface, but handling suffers a little with their being enclosed. Astern power is likely to be reduced because of the restriction in the flow of water for'ard from the prop, affecting stopping, and the turning circle of twin screws will be increased due to the skeg effect at the stern. Paddlewheel effect will also be less, due to the tunnel shielding the side of the prop.

Index

Major topic references are listed beneath each chapter heading in the Contents list. This Index is designed to complement these sub-headings by providing, for each subject listed below, further references that may be found elsewhere in the book. (*Page numbers in italics refer to illustrations or captions*)